MW01171765

Mommypreneur

"How to raise your babies AND your bank account, and enjoy the journey while you do it"

Autrina Tillman

Co-Authors

Michael Shepherd Jr

Micah Shepherd

DEDICATION

This book is dedicated to my lifelines. Michael (VJ) and Micah, you are my why, my reason, my cause, my air, my heartbeats, my peace, my laughter, my joy, my everything. My desire to be, to exist, and to escape continued because of you. The Most High blessed me with fuel for the fire; you are my fuel. I want you to know that I have your front, back, top, bottom, and both sides as long as there's breath in my body. And I will become a part of your ancestral covering even after this natural lifetime expires.

Table of Contents

ACKNOWLEDGMENTS

I want to thank all the inspirational women of the world. My "how to be a woman" handbook came from My Creator and My Feminine Examples of a boss. From Grandmothers to little princesses and everything between, powerful women (especially melanated ones) have been abundant and in focus. I've been inspired much of my life watching the resilience of mothers, female entrepreneurs, educators, wives, athletes, writers, inventors, and survivors. Mommies everywhere are raising children alone, through the friction and dysfunction of a current or past relationship or tag-teaming in a healthy situation with Dad. Either way, the most common statistics show how Mommies figure it out, sacrifice themselves and get shit done by any means necessary. Great job, Queens!

Introduction

This book contains a handbook about how to successfully be a Mommy and a business owner. Well, that sounded good, but since there is definitely no one-size-fits-all handbook, I'll just tell you a little about what I believe and how it has worked for me. I was a single mom for most of my children's childhood, and I've been an entrepreneur the entire time; like 100% commission; like if I don't work, we don't eat; like it doesn't matter if I have a migraine because there are 2 conference calls today; like if no one can watch the kids, they will be my 5 and 6-year-old assistants today; like I'm not missing my son's baseball game so I have to do cram all of my life insurance appointments in before 5; like I had to fill out every scholarship and financial aid application early to make sure I never had to tell my kids no about a desire that could make them great in the future, or just something fun; Like I had late meetings today, but my daughter is self-conscious about her hair; so we were not going to bed until I've created the cutest natural style for her to feel beautiful at school tomorrow. Like It doesn't matter if I'm exhausted; they are my why and I can't make excuses and money, so I chose the latter. Let me give you an example: One time, I had a life insurance appointment, and it had already been a very busy day! My tire had popped and gone flat about a block away from my client's home. This was a big appointment that would end in about a $4,000 commission check with about 2 hours of work. I was overwhelmed, but it only lasted about 5 minutes because my rule of thumb was that I could always give myself grace and take 5. I cried a little, maybe screamed once or twice, and ended my tantrum with a gratitude prayer because I actually made it to the house on my flat tire, and I was about to go in here and conquer this appointment. So, I went in, greeted my clients, and told them that I had allergies because I was sure that my eyes were still glassy and red. Needless to say, I successfully helped the clients and bagged my $4,000 commission. It was late, like 11 pm late, so I happily went back to my car, drove around the corner away from their home, and called roadside assistance to change my tire. It was a good night.

(Home, 2022) "-Out of 11,016,000 single parent families in the U.S., 80% are single mothers. 52.9% of single mothers are millennials. 15.6 million children live in single mother households in the U.S. 52.3% of single mothers have never been married, 29.3% are divorced."

"-71% of mommypreneurs still serve as the primary childcare provider."

"-Women own about 43% of small businesses in the U.S., which is almost 14 million businesses. When you combine all the women-owned businesses, they are generating about $1.9 trillion per year. That's a lot of money supporting the economy!"

"-1 in 3 women-owned businesses is owned by a mom. That translates to almost 4.7 million businesses."

For as long as I can remember, people would always say, "Trina, your kids are so amazing. What did you do? How did you raise them? How do you get them to act the way they act?" And it was a weird question to me, so I would always just humbly say, "They've just always been this way. They've always been very well-mannered, accountable, intelligent, grateful, and leaders."

I found myself constantly talking about parenting with my friends, associates, and sometimes just passersby. I've had conflict resolution conversations and been asked many questions about my methods of discipline. I've gotten into long and extensive conversations about school and education and how my kids get such good grades.

I've had many conversations about extracurricular activities and how I make them participate. That's always been a weird question because I've never had to make them participate or be interested in anything.

I've gotten the "How did you make them be so well mannered?" question and the "How do you make them so interested in going to school?" question. As my kids have grown older, people have questioned me about how we are still so close. And especially my son, because he still wants to be up under me all the time. People constantly point out how ambitious they are and how they work so diligently to accomplish their goals.

Until well into high school, my children had never asked me for a pair of high-priced brand-name shoes or a typical game system that most children ask for. This wasn't because I steered them in the direction of not asking or even because they wouldn't have probably gotten those things had they requested them. My children usually ask for money to explore their craft or interest, which aided the progression of their gifts and talents as they grew older. Again, I never told them directly that they had to go this route. And I never even thought about the fact that they subconsciously did until they were much older, and I was questioned about it.

Good energy, gratefulness, and the idea of manifestation have always been a part of my DNA. I didn't really understand what it was or all the technical terms when I was younger, but as I got older, hung around the right people, and studied, I began to realize more and more that the law of attraction was really real.

I didn't insist that my children be interested in any particular thing or anything materialistic. However, I raised them in an environment synonymous with my belief system. And I never told them to do as I said, I always challenged them to pay attention to what I do.

The more I was asked questions about my parenting style, and the older my children got, the more I realized that all their behaviors were based on their mindset. It was all based on what their subconscious mind had been soaking up since birth or even before birth. It's very hard to explain unless you dig deep into the subconscious mind, ego, conscious mind, and the law of attraction.

The older my children got, I also began to see their mindset and their upbringing work with practical matters. As they began to make young adult decisions, I saw the lessons at work. The more I saw them do as I do and not only as I say as they made more and more adult decisions, I realized that this stuff really worked.

How to be a mommy does not come with a handbook, and I have proudly and sometimes critically watched moms attempt to do the best that they know possible when it comes to raising brilliant children.

I definitely have not done everything perfectly, but because of my innate abilities from The Most High, I finally came to the same conclusion as those around me. I am qualified to compose a pretty good handbook. I'm sure this book doesn't have all the answers, or maybe not even most of the answers. But I promise if you catch on to any portion of the insight given, it will move you ahead a little more smoothly in some areas of parenting and entrepreneurship. Moms are already superheroes, and my hope is that Mommypreneur helps your cape to stay a little cleaner.

Chapter 1
Grandparents

Don't she get a biscuit with that pickle? This is what my 80-year-old grandmother asked the convenient store cashier after she opened up the pickle jar, put the big green pickle in the plastic baggie, and handed it over the counter to me. "No," Grand nanny, I said, "they don't give you biscuits at the corner store." "Well, what do they think you're supposed to do, just eat the pickle by itself?"

My grandmother, in my opinion, was a perfect build for an almost 70-year-old. She was healthy and proportioned well. She stood about five foot six, and if I had to guess, I would say 175 pounds. My grandmother was brown-skinned and had processed hair for most of what I remember. I think she had natural hair for a season too, and she would straighten it or press it with a hot comb.

My grandmother had a perfect set of freckles on her face, and she actually had freckles all over her body from a slight case of vitiligo. I actually inherited the vitiligo from my grandmother, and one of the things that makes me remember her all the time is when I look down at my legs and see the little white spots that are mostly invisible to others if they are not looking for them intentionally.

She wore glasses, and her smile is ingrained in my mind. When she would smile, it would be a big smile and very distinctive in a way that lets you know that she was happy with life for the most part. My grandmother was pretty active for her age as well, so she mostly wore britches, as she would call them, which would just be called pants by the average person. And she usually had on a button-up shirt or sometimes just a t-shirt. When she wore button-up shirts, she would usually have the sleeves rolled up, and because she was always working in the garden or going fishing, sometimes she also had her pant legs rolled up.

Another vivid memory about my grandmother was when she wasn't dressed for the garden, cutting grass, fishing, or going to town to order groceries, she would be dressed for church. My grandmother ushered most Sundays, so I clearly remember the white usher's dress and the white usher's shoes, along with the white gloves that she would have on, especially on communion Sundays. My grandmother was very committed to her church duties, and she dressed the part very well. I'm pretty sure my grandmother was the first person to teach me that it is appropriate to wear a slip underneath your church attire so that you couldn't see through your dress and that it was appropriate to wear pantyhose with your dress as well.

My Grandmother was one of my lifelines growing up, and in her 80-year-old South Carolina home-grown way, she taught me to always expect more.

I grew up knowing that there was so much that I had to offer this world and that I was destined for greatness; I was blessed to have great people in my life, even as a child. And I discovered that the bloodline that came before me included some powerful, confident, and persevering melanated Kings and Queens!

I always became a sponge in every environment, and each environment shaped me to be who I am continuing to become in this lifetime.

Because of trauma, some of my childhood memories are not as vivid as they should be. Counseling has taught me that they are suppressed as my brain's way of protecting my mental. For more information on this, stay tuned for my next book............

But what I do remember is just as powerful. Let me introduce you to a few of the pivotal players in my game of life.

We chatted a little about one of my Grandmothers at the beginning of the chapter. Growing up, my Grandparents were the most influential, nurturing, supportive, molding examples of excellence that I've ever witnessed. They taught me respect; how to give it and how to expect it! If you walked past our house and didn't speak, you would be invited to the porch for a lesson. When we woke up in the morning, greeting everyone in the house was the protocol before starting our day, just some good old fashion values. I can remember being on my Grand nanny's hip at 5 years old, learning how to make biscuits from scratch. The ingredients included what she called clabbered milk (similar to buttermilk), lard, flour, wait..... I can't reveal all the goodness. Oh, the food was so delicious in those days! The dinner spread would be laid with collard greens, green beans, macaroni and cheese, fried chicken, turkey, ham, dressing, cornbread, yams, rice and gravy, cranberry sauce, and more goodness that I know I'm forgetting. I also remember growing most of our vegetables in the garden. At a very young age, I helped to hoe, till, and plant. Now I know why I was so healthy and in tune with the earth because my Grandmother had me grounded since I was a toddler. Apple trees and blackberry vines are also among my favorite memories as a child. My cousins and I would spend entire days playing and stopping every so often to pick blackberries, and there were lots of them. You had to remember to wash the chiggers off the blackberries, but of course, we would sometimes just wipe them with our clothes and pop them in our mouths; bugs and all! The fresh fruits growing on the trees and vines were so tasty and refreshing. We would bring blackberries back by the bags full, and grand nanny would make delicious blackberry pies.

My grandmother would take me fishing weekly. We fished with cane poles and worms. I would take the worm out of the bucket and feed it on the hook, of course, with grand nanny's supervision. It would wiggle and squirm, but that bothered me none. I remember being around 8 years old and catching a 5lb bass. My grandmother had to help me pull it out of the water, which was probably my biggest catch. She raved about that catch and boosted my head up for years to come. "Baby, you remember when you caught that big fish that almost pulled you into the water?" Still, to this day, I tell that story from time to time, and my friends and family just laugh. I also remember several fishing trips that involved snakes. We would see snakes from time to time, and they would not move Grand nanny at all. She would simultaneously fish, retrieve her pocketknife and perfectly cut the head off a snake that was in close proximity. The movement was fluid, and she was unbothered. I have seen her do this on more than 1 occasion.

Other memories worth sharing are the stories. My grandfather was my story time partner. My pop was a tall, dark and handsome black man. He stood about six foot two to six foot three if I had to guess, about 220 pounds, and he was everything that you can imagine in a chocolate King. My pop was confident and proud and thought highly of himself, just short of conceited. He would smile so big, leaving a smirk on his face. From the time I met him until the time he passed, I don't remember there being many, if any, wrinkles on his face. His skin was smooth, and his features were dominant. My pop was a dresser. My favorite thing about his attire was the many hats he kept on top of the dresser, hanging on the mirror, and at the top of his closet in his room. He very seldom dressed down. When he was doing his carpentry work or yard work, you may see him in a pair of Dickies pants, slacks, and a t-shirt or a button-down shirt with the sleeves rolled up, but I mostly saw him dressed up. He almost always had on a suit, a full suit, or some slacks and a button-down shirt, and his suits were never complete without his hat, period. My grandfather was known for his hats, and I was interested in wearing hats because of him. From a very young age, I began to admire them, and I would ask him if I could have the hats that got old, the ones that he didn't want anymore. I would take his hats off his head and play in the mirror like they were mine, and every once in a while, I would bribe him into giving me one of his hats. My grandfather almost always had on hard bottom shoes, mostly Stacy Adams. My grandfather was always dressed for a night on the town or the best-looking deacon in the church, and I am sure that some of my fashion sense and confidence in my appearance were inherited from him.

He worked a lot and was always out and about, but I could always seem to catch him long enough to tell me the most intriguing, historical, or just exciting stories that he could conjure up. I would catch him in the shed doing carpentry work, or on the couch trying to watch Andy Griffith, or in the kitchen making homemade mac and cheese (yes, my Pops could burn too), and I would learn amazing things about my ancestors, civil rights, political parties, and just good old fashion values. I would take it all in and put in my memory bank to add to my greatness on life's journey. One of the stories that he told me about my grandmother recently reiterated some facts. My great great grandfather was able to purchase 400 acres of land in South Carolina many years ago. This was in the 1800s, so I don't need to give you a lesson on the treatment and opportunities of black and brown people in that era. He grew up with a white boy that remained his friend into their adulthood and offered to sell these 400 acres to him. My great great grandfather was a hard worker, and he used some of the money that he had saved up to purchase this land. My grandmother recently told me that the land was about $1 per acre, which was a lot of money at the time. When he passed on, my great-grandmother inherited the land. She was the only child and had the entire fortune with no idea just how much of a fortune it was. My family had livestock and land, and because we were not educated beyond the innate genius that we were born with, we had no idea what that could mean for generations to come. My great-grandmother sold all the land except for 130 acres before she passed on. My last memory of her was before the age of 10. She was a tall light skinned big boned lady, and her personality was nothing short of confident. My grandfather took charge of the land after his mother passed and eventually decided to sell it and split the proceeds among his siblings. He got 100,000+ dollars for the land but regretted the decision later. My grandfather learned much more about land, real estate, and how money works as he got older and educated himself. He said if he had to do it all over, he would not have sold all the land back then. I understand how oppression and history took away our ability to make the best generational decisions in those days, and some of that still lingers today. However, it makes me proud and grateful to have the ancestral bloodline I have. The decision of my great great grandfather to acquire the land and the natural progression of my amazing family with no real knowledge of what to do is what makes me who I am today. We were millionaires and didn't even know it, so now is the time for the manifestation of what always was!

Church; Growing up in the south makes church an inevitable memory. Again, starting with my grandparents, I was in church all day every Sunday and at least one other day during the week. I was in Sunday School and at Bible Study regularly. My fondest memories include eating at church after any special anniversary or event and the many choirs that I've sang on. Singing was by far my favorite part of church, and it remained to be my biggest involvement well into my adulthood. I've been on numerous children's choirs, young adult choirs, adult choirs, and mass choirs. I'm an alto. A very strong alto, if I must say, and I absolutely love singing harmonies, melodies, and minors, exploring the art of music! I've been a choir leader, a praise and worship leader, and a member of the Winston-Salem State University Gospel Choir. I must give credit to my church families and gospel music as I talk about any success on this journey of life.

I've had many different experiences with church because my paternal grandparents were Presbyterian, and my two maternal grandmothers were Baptist and Holiness. I attended church with all of them, so I must say that I'm definitely classified growing up as "a church girl."

I have been blessed to be in the presence of 4 grandmothers and 1 grandfather in my lifetime, and at 44 years old, my paternal grandmother is still here with me, and her comforting voice still brings me joy!

Chapter 2
Gastonia

Yep, you heard me! I was shaped and molded in the Gas House. So, all my grandparents except one were only about an hour away from where My Mother decided to make our home in Gastonia, NC. (Home, n.d.). "Gastonia is the largest city in and the county seat of Gaston County, North Carolina, United States. It is the second-largest satellite city in the Charlotte area, behind Concord. The population was 80,411 at the 2020 Census, up from 71,741 in 2010. Gastonia is the 13th most populous city in North Carolina. The City Hospital-Gaston Memorial Hospital, Craig Farmstead, Downtown Gastonia Historic District, First National Bank Building, Gaston County Courthouse, Gastonia High School, David Jenkins House, Loray Mill Historic District, Robinson-Gardner Building, Third National Bank Building, and William J. Wilson House are listed on the National Register of Historic Places. The city is known for textiles, and a place like Crowders Mountain State Park is located west of the city, near Kings Mountain. The park offers a number of hiking trails, as well as campgrounds, picnic areas, rock climbing, and fishing. This is a very popular park and a great place to exercise and experience great mountain top scenery."

I was about elementary school age when we first settled in Gastonia, and this book is not my autobiography, so the purpose of this chapter is just to tell you about a few of the people or other influences that I would be remiss if I didn't mention.

I went to Rhyne Elementary School, and the first teacher that I remember ended up being my favorite and most memorable throughout my entire educational experience. Ms. Hardin, my 3rd grade teacher, was the sh---. She was everything; about 5'6" with smooth chocolate skin, and she had a prissy but stern personality that exudes confidence. She expected greatness and would not accept anything less. I took to her immediately because she was the teacher that would love on, nurture, educate, feed, encourage and praise you consistently. But she would also beat your ass like you were hers if you got out of line. I was a great student, and some may have even called me the teacher's pet. I was a straight-A student in her class, but just like now, I talked excessively. I had something to say about everything, and I would take on the role of teacher's assistant without being asked. I would attempt to answer all the questions during classroom discussions, and Ms. Hardin would tell me to let someone else have a chance to answer sometimes. I was always talking out of turn or attempting to be a counselor to one of my classmates at an inappropriate time. My report card would always have a row of A's but be tainted with a U for unsatisfactory in the conduct section. I was a very good student overall, and this U was strictly because I talked too much. Ms. Hardin would call my mom and rave about how smart I was and how I was one of her best students, but the conversation would eventually lead to a collaboration of how to make me keep my mouth shut at inappropriate times. Don't get me wrong, being talkative was great in a lot of instances, and my teachers could always count on me to keep the class progressive. And although I had to mature and get a grip on when to use my voice, I learned quickly that talking is my gift; I have used it and will use it for the rest of my days to be the change that My creator placed me here to be. I've always known that I was different, created for signs and wonders, and she co-signed that reality, regularly telling me just how brilliant I was. She never expected anything mediocre from me, and she treated me like one of her own. Ms. Hardin has been a staple in the community since before I was her 3rd grade student, and she is still as beautiful and vibrant as ever at her wise age. I actually spoke at an event in Gastonia recently, and roughly 33 years later, she showed up for me!

Another staple of Gastonia was Erwin Center. This was and still is not only a community center but an escape, an outlet, freedom, mentorship, fellowship, fun, and a constant. (Wikipedia Gastonia, NC) The Erwin Community Center offers programs that include, but are not limited to:

- Youth athletics
- Adult athletics
- Summer camps
- Senior citizen programs and group trips
- Card playing groups
- Youth cooking classes
- Youth leadership development
- Teen leadership clubs
- Babysitting and first aid classes
- Special events

"Erwin Center opened in 1961 on 15 acres in the Highland neighborhood of northern Gastonia. The center was named in honor of Dr. Herbert Erwin. Dr. Erwin was Gaston County's first African American physician and was well-known as an advocate for youth sports and activities. The early center housed a game room, meeting room, kitchen, lounge, and offices. The outdoor facilities included a football - baseball field, and playground. A full-size gymnasium was added in 1967, along with an outdoor basketball court. In 1989-90 a Gaston County Branch library was added. This project was a joint venture between the City's Community Development Department and Gaston County Public Library. Today, the park's outdoor facilities also include a swimming pool, a splash pad (open during the summer months), a grass volleyball court, horseshoe pits, a playground, a tot play area, a large picnic shelter, and a walking track. During the summer of 2020, a Black Lives Matter mural was painted on the Erwin Center basketball court by Ezekiel Clay, Jr."

I have so many memories that we could talk about, but one of my biggest is when they made me the scorekeeper/clock girl at the basketball games. I attended Highland Jr High School, and I would go to softball practice, go home and check-in, and then walk about a mile to the Erwin Center. I would usually get my siblings ready and take them with me to the center. This was a great place for us to bond. And since my mom worked a lot, I could have my teenage fun while babysitting because there was plenty at the center to keep them busy and excited. It was just my little brother (who is 5 years younger) and I until I was almost 15 years old, and we got a baby sister. My siblings and I were very close growing up, and I was definitely their second mom. Shad, and Cierra; were my first "why" outside of myself. I wanted to protect them and teach them everything that I was learning about this thing called life. I tried to be the best example possible growing up, and I can confidently say that I succeeded at that goal. My siblings are still two of the best additions to this Universe, and their footprints are growing daily.

The Center would host basketball leagues and tournaments regularly, and they would have volunteers to run the clock and keep score. I loved it! I love meeting new people and being in the mix, so this was right up my alley. I also loved basketball, so I played there often as well. I learned how to politic and network, and I also got the entrepreneurial bug early on just chatting with older people that had or were building businesses. I'm pretty nosey unapologetically, and I don't forget things that create growth or success, so I've always soaked up information whether someone was talking directly to me or I was eavesdropping on a conversation that they were having with someone else. Mr. Ferguson, Mrs. McClure, and Pete were the people that made everything tic for us as youth hungry for leadership in the community. "Mr. Ferguson had many accomplishments during his long tenure at the center, and his greatest was the fulfillment of his vision to build the library. It became the James Ferguson Branch of Gaston County Library." They were the glue that made everything stick, and they ran the center with pride!

I met Crick at Erwin Center. That's what everyone called him, but his name is Chris Adams. Crick is about 6 feet tall with an average build. He is brown-skinned with a head full of hair and usually a full beard. Crick always had on a hat, and he was either dressed for work, to work on a car, or to coach a sport. He was very relaxed and down to earth and loved by all the kids. He was always there coaching, mentoring, and just making sure that the young people were ok. He has a heart of gold, and because I'm always in the mix, I was always around soaking up whatever knowledge or lesson was being given. He would answer all my questions and was very patient anytime any of us needed anything. He became something like my Godfather, and I ended up meeting his family. He, his lovely wife, and his children became part of my extended family, and this is a bond that I will forever cherish. I learned everything from how I should expect a young man to treat me to how to change brake pads on a car, and so much in between, which I will save for a future book.

Christ Community Baptist Church was right around the corner from our apartment. This is the church that I attended for most of my youth in Gastonia. I was there a lot! My family would go together, or sometimes, I would just walk to church alone and participate in whatever was going on at the time. The pastor and the first family of the church were also my family. We were cousins, and I absolutely love them. Reverend Mac is what we all called the pastor. Some of the most genuine people you will ever meet, and I know that The Most High put us right there in that season by divine appointment. Remember, I'm a church girl and music "kept" me through most of my life, so of course, I was in the choir. Tim was our choir director, and he was about that life! To this day, I've never seen anyone as animated and unapologetic on them keys! If you couldn't sing, you figured out if Tim had anything to do with it. He made you feel like you were Shirley Caesar or Rance Allen with that microphone. Our choir even had the opportunity to go sing on a very popular gospel music TV show called Bobby Jones Gospel. We were something like celebrities, and we did our appearance much justice. We sang our hearts out, making our choir director, pastor, congregation, and most of all, OUR CREATOR proud! In choir rehearsal, we would sing, shout, dance, cry, praise, and just have a hallelujah good time! It was one of my favorite times of the week. I led several songs; my favorite being one called Power. (♫♫♫) Power, power, Holy Ghost, Power…….. Seemed like we sang that song for an entire hour each time. I would shout and dance every time I sang it. I've always been overwhelmed with gratitude, even from a young age. I've always expected greatness and knew that I was put here for just that, so gratitude is a constant in my life. If you know that everything that you desire is already yours, gratitude is a bit subconscious. I met many of my childhood friends in church, and many of them are still my friends or, at the very least, associates to this day. I have some very fond memories of that season, and I actually met my very best friend of most of my adolescent and young adult and early adult years, right there at good ole Christ Community Baptist Church.

Chapter 3
Bestie

You always have a little more courage and tenacity when
you have a best friend to multiply your joy
and divide your sorrows.
Autrina

We were two peas in a pod, and we both absolutely loved singing and being in the mix! We would stand side by side as we sang our many duets, or she would stand on one end of the choir and me on the other so that our very strong alto voices would balance out the section. We shouted and danced hand in hand as we used our praises for healing and rejoicing service after service. We were involved in every youth event or assignment and took our ministry responsibilities seriously. Church was in our DNA.

She is a Libra, and I am a Gemini; two air signs that believe in going with the flow or changing it up when necessary to make our world go round. Even when we went to different schools, we always seemed to find each other after school and on most weekends. The story of our life is another book, but I will let you in on a couple of fun and exciting experiences we had.

What's her name? Oh, it's Nickie, at least that's what her friends and family called her. She was about 5'5" with a cute, slim build. She was a lighter complexion, and she was outgoing and confident! She was a Mama Bear and, like me, the oldest of her siblings. Nikki was there for a lot of firsts; The first time I went to a Boys and Girls Club dance, the first time I went to the Waffle House in Charlotte, NC., and the first time I visited a college or University.

Let me tell you about these Boys and Girls Club dances and any other dance or party event we could infiltrate. We were dancing machines! We would make up routines and put on qualified dancing attire with the intention of stealing every show. This was the baggy era and the daisy duke's era. We usually had on some baggy pants or overalls with one of the straps down. We wore button-up dress shirts, and I even found a necktie every so often. We participated in the dance contests and might as well have been Tisha Campbell and A.J. Johnson in the dance battle on House Party! Reggae, to this day, is still my absolute favorite music to dance to. I remember my mother getting calls after a Patra-inspired dance-off. I think the song was "Queen of the Pack," and we might as well have been in Kingston, Jamaica, at a reggae dancehall performing! We gave the people every Jamaican-inspired whine and grind needed to come out on top! My mom said they asked if she was aware of me grinding and doing dances that required me to end up going down to the floor. Too funny…. We concluded that whoever was inquiring was just jealous that they were not young enough or skilled enough to still do the most popular dances at the time.

Then it was that time we went to the Waffle House, and I knew young adulthood was upon me. I don't even remember our initial reason for going to Charlotte, but I do remember that the adults spoke of Charlotte as the city, which was supposed to be dangerous. Charlotte was bigger, and there may have been a club shooting or two that made Gastonians see it as a war zone. To my recollection, we only lived about 20 minutes from Charlotte, and I had never been there. It was like our poverty; boxed mentality had trapped us in the walls of this little rural town. Not only did we go to the Waffle House, but it was late. (Sidenote: Waffle House is a small restaurant that everyone goes to in the middle of the night after the club. They have one grill that all of the food is cooked on, and if you've never experienced it, it's worth putting on your bucket list.) We arrived at the Waffle house after our Charlotte event, and it was just like I'd heard. There were people hanging out in front of the restaurant just chillin' and talking. There were cars parked with the doors open and music playing. It was mostly adolescents and young adults congregating, and most appeared to have on "going out" attire. The short skirts and dresses, heals or sandals, and flashy jewelry gave it away. You could smell a few different fragrances of smoke, such as cigars, cigarettes, and even some marijuana smoke mixed in throughout the parking lot. This experience was so exciting, and I felt my adolescence in full effect! We did actually get a table and eat eventually, and I ordered what I still order to this day. A patty melt plate with no onions or bacon and hashbrowns covered (that means with cheese on top). Waffle house is still the to-go-to spot when it's too late, and everything else is closed.

Another honorable mention would be University Day at A&T State University. Everyone was excited about going to visit this HBCU and being amid the life that was in our near future. We were planning and plotting before the bus took off, and even better, we had some friends that had already matriculated at the University and could show us around. The drive was exciting as we sang, chatted, and listened to the agenda and the rules to follow once we were on campus. The most important instructions were how to find the bus and what time to find the bus once the outing was over.

We were off. There were seminars, tours, entertainment, and everything you can imagine demonstrating the life of a college student. At some point during the field trip, we were free to move about and explore as we pleased. It started to rain pretty hard, so Nikki and I capitalized on that freedom and found the dorm room of our friends. They were listening to music and playing cards, and they welcomed us to join them. During the card game and all the fun, the storm got worse, and we were just happy to be inside. Needless to say, we lost track of time and, at some point, noticed that we had extended our visit beyond the instructed "meet back at the bus" time. Oh shit!!! We looked at each other and ran out to find the bus, and the bus was gone. Time stood still as we panicked and decided whose mother would be the least destructive when we shared that we had got left in Greensboro, NC. This is hilarious now, but I promise it was far from funny in 1995. Well, the short story is we figured it out, and we made it out unscathed. Other than the bus incident, this HBCU visit was very impactful, and I landed at Winston-Salem State University, where I graduated in the year 2000 with a bachelor of science in Biology and Chemistry. Nikki and I had a way of making life light and optimistic despite any hardships or inconsistencies it threw us at our young impressionable ages. We were fixers, movers, and shakers, and nothing could steal our joy. She continued to be there for a lot of firsts and big events, including my college graduation, and I will forever be grateful. Her support came during an important part of my existence, and it far surpassed friendship.

Chapter 4
Winston-Salem, NC

I never lose; I either win or I learn.
Nelson Mandela

Whether something happens that you perceive as good, bad, or indifferent, you should soak up the lesson. Failure has several definitions; perspective and mindset will determine how it affects you. A few definitions are the omission of occurrence or performance and lack of success or falling short. Failure is never final unless you quit on your journey, so FAIL BIG! This assures that your journey is only progressing to higher heights each time you set out. And focus on the victories that come from the failures. If you are learning every time, victories are inevitable. The next time something challenging happens to you, consider it a gift and allow it to catapult you to the next level.

Just in case you haven't noticed, I am sharing with you what some of my most memorable influences and support looked like molding me into the Mommypreneur that I've become.

I decided on Winston-Salem State University. The acceptance letter was the start of an exciting 4 years to come. I was leaning towards the healthcare field because I enjoyed participating in

(HOSA) Health Occupation Students of America in high school. I wasn't completely sure what direction to go in, but I was absolutely sure that if it got me out of Gastonia, I had tunnel vision, and my speedometer was at a steady 100mph. I had a plan to be great, and absolutely nothing was going to stop me.

I was still a church girl then, so of course, the first things I attracted were other students and organizations associated with religion or spirituality. And my favorite thing in the world was still singing, so I quickly found the Winston-Salem State Gospel Choir. I met a lot of my college friends and associates by way of the choir, and I still keep in touch with many of them today. I also found my church home very quickly alongside some of the friends I grew fond of in our first semester of college. Growing up in Gastonia was pretty rough at times, and decompressing is an understatement when it comes to how big the exhale was once I got away. I know that the last sentence is loaded, but it reads exactly the way my heart felt it.

Cleveland Avenue Christian Church became my safe haven and remained a huge part of my life for over 10 years. Many leaders and members, especially the elders and wise counsel, taught us morals, values, and steadfastness when it comes to gratitude, manifestation, and revelation. As usual, I immediately got involved in every aspect that pertained to my age and place in the ministry. With the leadership of our Youth Pastor, a few of my classmates and some other youth joined together to strengthen the youth and college ministries. We had a praise and worship team, young adult choir, step team, dance ministry, and an array of other activities that kept us involved and aspiring to do good. We grew into mature adults along the way, and most of us are still flourishing and contributing positively to society today! Of course, there are many imperfections and discrepancies when we talk about religion, but I learned about spiritual relationship in those years. This later allowed me the ability to omit everything that no longer made sense and attach myself forever to the spiritual abilities and discernments that I was purposed for in this lifetime. Taking nothing away from my experience in that season, the church, later known as Greater Cleveland Avenue Christian Church, was my foundation and grounding for a mentality of magnitude and my "ask and you shall receive" lifestyle. I have always practiced the "eat the chicken and spit out the bone" concept, and there I got nutrition that would feed me for a lifetime on this journey.

There's another honorable mention in my heart that has always been with me through my expectation of success and greatness. I got a job shortly after graduation teaching 8th grade science and math at Hill Magnet School. This was considered a high-risk school, and it was interesting, to say the least. I love learning and teaching. Education and literacy have always been a passion, and it makes me all warm inside to know that I just taught someone something that could positively impact them for the rest of their lives and generations to come. These 8th graders were challenging, and some came from humble beginnings and harsh lifestyles. However, this was one of the most rewarding assignments of my life. I was a teacher, mother, counselor, mentor, nurturer, and provider, and I could go on and on. Each day was a new challenge and a new victory, and Ms. Lajoi Wilson-Moore was a part of the glue that held it all together. She was the vice principal, and She was one of my first examples of a melanated Queen leading with poise and integrity. She was no pushover and easy by no means, but she was the epitome of standing firm in your confidence and your calling! Days that I grew weary or discouraged, I would see her in passing and remember what I was capable of accomplishing. I'm unsure if she had any idea of her impact on furthering my expectation of greatness. But I could not move forward without honoring her.

During my short teaching stint, I was met with the greatest experience to date (other than the birth of my beautiful Children) that originated in Winston-Salem. I was 26 years old when I was introduced to a young couple that looked like me and came from where I came from, making about 250k/year. All I wanted to know was where do I go and what do I do to copy whatever blueprint they were following. If it was legal and positive, I was down. I had been speaking, believing, and manifesting my entire life. Before I even knew what I was doing, my subconscious mind had already been created to attract and believe. That childlike innocent expectation for the Universe to give me whatever I want has never diminished. They taught me financial concepts like the "Rule of 72" and what saving $100 a day would do from the age of 25 to 65. It was starting to make sense. Being wealthy and successful wasn't just something that other people could attain. That burning desire that I had my entire life was about to develop some wings and circle the galaxy.

Every encounter in life, some small and some great, has a purpose and an impact on your journey. Soak up every lesson, focus on the journey, and the destination will take care of itself.

Autrina

Before anything ever presents itself physically, it must first develop in your mind.

Autrina

Now we should get into some of the huge influence that came from this meeting and the Mindset work that you need to ever accomplish the greatness that you were created for.

Chapter 5
Mentorship

A smart man makes a mistake, learns from it, and never makes
that mistake again. But a wise man finds a smart man
and learns from him how to avoid the
mistake altogether.
Roy H. Williams

The part of the meeting that impacted my life the most started and continued with mentorship. I quickly obtained the knowledge of how to accept and receive mentorship and why it would change my life forever. Great minds think alike is a simple but powerful cliché. I was suddenly surrounded by wealth and leadership in every direction, and the most interesting part was many of my mentors had a similar or more challenging upbringing than me. And I must mention that many of them looked like me.

Mentorship is extremely important. You can get anywhere faster with guidance. Think about the development of a child. No matter how innately brilliant they are, there still must be guidance from the small steps to them reaching milestones. Hindsight is 20/20, and, in many instances, mentorship can be your hindsight. How much easier would starting out with 20/20 be?

Have you ever traveled down a dark road for the first time in a new city or town? If it's curvy or uncommonly shaped, it could be tricky and, if not careful, could even lead to an accident.

2 Lessons

Be humble. Just because you're a good driver doesn't mean you won't need to slow down and learn this road.

If you are traveling with a local, you could ride with them and let them guide you through the road pattern to get there safely the first time. Afterward, you are comfortable doing it alone.

Now I'm sure you may have eventually gotten through it alone, but with all the anxiety and mistakes that could have been avoided with guidance. If you don't understand, try training someone smart to do something you have already mastered. You will see mistakes that they make time and time again that they would have avoided by just being humble at first as you held their hand.

Leaders have mentors, Coaches have coaches, counselors have counselors, and one of the greatest reasons for failure is trying to do it alone. I'm not saying that trial and error is never necessary, but guided trial and error is proven to be much more productive. Mentorship has no limit, and it doesn't have to be someone you know. It could be face-to-face, virtual, in a book, etc. Mentors could be teachers, managers, family, peers, or anyone that make you realize your potential. Get you a mentor!

My mentors introduced me to the law of attraction and manifestation in a way that made me realize my power and ability to literally change my life. I remember the first time I watched "The Secret"; it blew my mind. It made everything that I'd ever learned in church come to life. It is simply the "Law of Attraction." Essentially, the law states that whatever consumes your thoughts is what you will eventually get in your life. So, if you think of all the things you don't want in your life, you'll only get the things you don't want. It explained why my intuition and my innate gift of manifestation weren't weird or out of place like they seemed to be my whole life. We've heard our whole life that faith is the substance of things hoped for, the evidence of things not seen. Let's go a little further. Belief is an acceptance that something is true or that it exists. If you believe it exists, then there's no need to hope for it. You will never achieve more than you believe because it's impossible to outperform your belief level.

How good are you willing to let your life become? Only your mindset can stop your progression.

Chapter 6
Let's talk Manifestation

I am a Spiritual Being, and because I'm connected to the source
of all that is, All that is possible is
possible for me!
-Oprah

The Universe is your playground! Christians tell you to ask, and you shall receive. The law of attraction says whatever you focus your energy on will come back to you. If you're a believer, it is already done, correct? So why do we spend our entire life wanting? The Universe gives us exactly what we ask for, whether it's out loud or in our minds. If you put the spirit of wanting out in the universe, you will always want. If you put the spirit of having out in the universe, you will always have. This may go over your head, but The law of Conservation of Energy states that energy cannot be created nor destroyed- only converted from one form of energy to another. AND Newton's third law states that for every action, there is an equal or opposite reaction. Everything is energy, so you literally control what happens in your life.

Manifestation is to create or turn something from an idea into a reality. It is the conscious creation of the circumstances and outcomes that make for a fulfilling life. This will eventually become subconscious, and I am living proof. Now I just expect greatness, and sometimes I even shock myself, like damn, you really believe that is your destiny; And myself is like, absolutely! Let me give you five steps to start your manifestation journey:

1. Know exactly what you ~~want~~ have! We are going to get rid of wanting because it's already created. We just must attract that energy back to us. Make your intentions as specific as possible. Don't give the Universe a mixed signal.

2. Ask for what you ~~want~~ have! I'll give you an example of how to do that shortly. It is most important to align yourself with the Universe, Your Creator, or whatever you believe in that's bigger than you. Remember, it's already created; you just must let the Universe know that you are expecting it and ready to receive it, and it will come to you. It's not your responsibility to figure out how just to align yourself and your expectations as you continue the journey. We should take many more notes from our kids because they expect what they desire. When you're walking through Walmart with your 4-year-old, and they say, "Mommy can we buy MY bike." They have already expected ownership before you even make the purchase. And they are going to remind you until you actually buy the bike or start to diminish their genuine, innate manifestation abilities by never buying the bike. The same way that a 4-year-old asked for the bike is how you ask the Universe to give you your desires. You can do it through prayer, meditation, visualization, speaking your intentions aloud, writing it

out, or whatever feels good to you. You just need to remember to do it in present tense and speak current existence. You can write; I have a 2-story house that is 6,000 square feet with 6 bedrooms and 5 ½ bathrooms. My home has granite countertops and hardwood floors, and high tray ceilings. It has a fireplace in the living room and Primary bedroom, and I have a lakeview in the rear of the house. It sits on 2 acres of land, and there's a below ground pool, and we have a basketball court, and so on…. You get the point. Now put a screen saver on a device you see daily, such as your computer monitor, that portrays your desired dream home. Your prayers should always be prayers of gratitude. Yah, I'm grateful for My new estate, my new Mercedes, and my six-figure increase in income. I'm grateful for my excellent health and my strong, healthy children. Thank you for our family vacation to the Caribbean that will create memories lasting a lifetime…. And so on. The point is everything that you put out alerts the Universe that you are ready to receive what is already created. Now again, you just continue your journey, being consistent in your prayers, visualizations, affirmations, etc., and watch the Universe work on your behalf.

This new enlightenment on manifestation isn't for the faint at heart. Most of us are reversing the way we've wanted and prayed our entire life. Practice makes permanent, so unless you practice this consistently, you won't start to believe it enough for it to actually work. I'm writing another book specifically about how to manifest, and I teach this in great detail to my coaching clients.

3. Manifestation is co-creating (a collaboration with the Universe), so you will not see results without action.

Remember, Faith or Belief without works is not going to allow fruition to take place. I once heard a story about a man trapped on his roof in flood. This man asked God to save him from the flood and get him off the roof. As the man was praying and crying, three boats went by in the flood waters. The man just sat on the roof and wallowed in his misery and distress as he feared dying on the roof. Later, he asked God why He didn't save him from the flood, and God told him that He sent three boats. All the man had to do was get on one of the boats, and he would have floated to safety. Don't sit on your roof wanting to be saved from the flood of lack. Put your desires and affirmations into the Universe, continue your journey and GET ON THE BOAT! Get a mentor or a coach, design a plan, create a routine, network with people, take a class, and do things that you don't currently do to get things that you currently don't have. Expect to attract what you want, but you have to put your mind in that space. Look up and research that vacation destination, go to the Mercedes Benz car lot, Go preview mansions, and hang out with people that have more than you. You must feel your goal, dreams, and desires daily before you ever hold the keys in your hand.

4. We talked about being grateful earlier. Gratitude is key. (King James Bible, n.d.)1 Thessalonians 5:16-17 says Rejoice evermore. Pray without ceasing. That means that you should be in a constant state of gratitude. Chapter 21 says Prove all things: hold fast that which is good. The Universe recognizes this as you accepting what was already created and destined for you. In the beginning, you have to reverse brainwash yourself into believing because you've been brainwashed your entire life to accept lack. Be grateful for everything, no matter how

big or small. Small victories prepare you to accept large victories, but you have to acknowledge them all. Again, this cultivates the Universe and says you are ready to receive more. You were able to pay a bill down or lower it. You found a dollar on the ground, you didn't eat any sweets today, you noticed that the cough you had for a week was now gone, your child made a good grade in school, the water was clear when you turned on the faucet, you were able to put your shoes on without assistance, your car started when you turned the key or pushed the button, I could literally go on for hours if I tried. Take 10 minutes before bed or upon rising every day to write down a few things that you're grateful for as well as anything that got you closer to your goals.

Write down limiting beliefs and replace them with reverse positive affirmations. The energy we put out in the world is the energy we get back. You can change your energy. Focus on activities and thoughts that create or cultivate feelings of joy and happiness. Meditate on your desires and what you are grateful for. Do yoga, donate to someone less fortunate, or volunteer once a week for a cause near and dear to you.

5. The last step is simple but critical. Trust the process! The process is fluid, so you can let yourself get discouraged. That is why consistency is so important. Your belief matters more than any other step. Trust your visions, desires, and actions, as well as the fact that your Creator or the Universe is aligning with you. Most people give up just before their breakthrough. Trust your instincts.

Don't fall back on anything, but instead, fail big and fail forward. If you hang around the barbershop long enough, you will eventually get a haircut.

Chapter 7
Developing the mind

Being a mommyprenuer and learning everything that we've talked about thus far is what has molded and shaped my brilliant children. I didn't have a handbook; I made many mistakes, and sometimes I had no clue if I was doing it right. But practicing all the principles and techniques above created a solid foundation for my parenting journey. In 2002 and 2003, my children immediately became my why. I was determined to create a positive, productive environment that would only breed success, belief, and an expectation of greatness. You must make this decision and don't turn back. The biggest assignment that I had was to live so that they were able to live by example. One of the most ignorant quotes that I hear parents tell their children is, "do what I say, not what I do." You are their blueprint; you are their safety, example, roadmap, inspiration, and foundation. Children are sponges; they walk because they see you walk. They eat because you pretended to eat with them and challenged them to copy you. They talk because they hear everyone around them talking. They even want to sit on your lap and drive because it looks fun and exciting when they watch you drive. Of course, they are going to do what you do. It seems very confusing that you would teach them by example in their most impressionable years and then at some point say, "Ok, forget that method and just do what I say." That is ludicrous, and if there's something that you don't want them to mimic, don't do it around them!

Being an entrepreneur and a mom taught me to teach them. Just to name a few, by example, I've been able to teach time management, patience, perseverance, the importance of ambition and self-determination, how to be a good follower, how to be a good leader, success, why mentorship is important, obedience, respect (giving and requiring) value, self-improvement, financial literacy, credit worthiness, gratitude, and being a Boss. One of the most important lessons has been not to sweat the small stuff (and everything is small stuff). Don't create unnecessary anxiety in your children that they will have to recover from as adults. The world will handle that for you. My rule of thumb is to take what I'm challenged with and decide if there could be a worst phone call at this moment to completely take my mind off my current dilemma. If the answer is yes, and it always is, then this challenge is classified as "small stuff." Your children will mimic how they see you handle life, so tread carefully. My kids have been in my personal and work environment from birth to young adulthood, and the goal has been to make it only a positive, productive, and joyful environment.

One thing that is superlative when it comes to teaching them how to think from the beginning is developing their subconscious mind. I'm talking about brainwashing them again. Remember that brainwashing is only negative if what you are being forced to believe is negative. If you leave that to the world, chances are your children will adopt questionable beliefs and practices that may not be in alignment with what you desired for them. Your beliefs and mindset affect what you allow in your life, and the Universe can give you whatever you desire. There are actually 3 minds, and it is imperative to understand how they work with energy, attraction, and manifestation. Most of us were not privy to appropriate conditioning as a child, so we have had to fight our way through the battle of the minds. The 3 minds are the subconscious, the ego, and the conscious mind. Let me explain. The subconscious is the part of your mind that notices and remembers information when you are not actively trying to do so and influences your behavior even though you do not realize it. Example: stop and think of a phone number or address from your childhood. Maybe it belonged to your grandmother, or it was your own. Now recite the number or address to yourself. You didn't have to look it up or look at the contacts in your phone. I remember my grandmother's phone number from my childhood, and she passed away in 2003. That's almost 20 years that I remember a number, and I have no control over the memory. It's just ingrained in my subconscious. Your subconscious is everything else after you understand your ego and your conscious mind, and it is exponentially more powerful than any other part of your mind, including your ego, once it's real. It is constant, and it will be who you are, whether you like it or not.

Your conscious mind is everything that you're aware and in control of. It's your willpower.

Let's talk about ego because this is the hang-up that most go a lifetime unaware of. When I say ego, you probably think of the commonly known definition describing arrogance and elevated self-interest. These definitions actually do coincide with the way ego truly plays an enormous part in our decision-making. It's actually the part of your mind that you use to cope with your surroundings and maintain a stable life. Your ego's sole purpose is to guarantee your survival, and it is stubborn enough to outlast your conscious mind. Everything you are doing now may not be the greatest, but you are alive. That job is only paying you $10/hr, but if you leave for a better opportunity, you may fail and lose them both. Then you could end up hungry and homeless. There's no way for your ego to know that changing your condition would make you better because right now, you are surviving. Even if the change is positive to your conscious mind, your ego doesn't differentiate because it only cares about survival. It's not interested in comfort or happiness, only survival. All it knows is whatever you've been doing thus far, including the struggle, is working to keep you alive. Your ego is what makes you fight anything different that you are learning right now as you read this book. It uses fear to keep you from adjusting or changing. Your conscious mind cannot beat your ego; therefore, you have to get beyond the change for your ego to adjust and no longer fight you on it.

The solution is your subconscious mind. Just as the ego is more powerful than your conscious, your subconscious leaps and bounds above your ego. Whatever you successfully convince your subconscious is no longer a threat and is rooted and grounded in your mind. It will activate the Universe to move you into matching circumstances without you realizing what is happening. Your subconscious is the energy that transfers and attracts everything around you to move in a way that manifests your desires. You won't always understand, but you don't need to. That's the job of The Most High or the Universe. Set your point of attraction with your subconscious and lead by example. This environment for your children will automatically lower the ego's level of resistance and train their subconscious. Giving well-placed instructions to their conscious mind and training their conscious means what would normally alert the ego will never even be a thing. This makes their journey much smoother and less resistant to growth. Life is supposed to feel good and be fun, and we have to change the narrative from the beginning.

Chapter 8
In the Womb and Beyond

*Consciousness is observing your thoughts and actions so that
you can live from true choice in the present moment
rather than being run by programming
from the past.*
Autrina

Before I start this chapter, I want to encourage and applaud all the phenomenal parents reading my book. You made it this far, and you are still demanding your destiny. Give yourself credit for all the victories as well as the lessons. We are failing forward, and this journey is worth the ride. If you are beyond any chapters as you read, just pick up where you are now in the journey.

In the womb.... create a safe space. Your child can immediately feel your energy, and it is automatically transferred to the growing fetus. I did not have a handbook, and I did not have much guidance, but my why was huge. Although I had some positive influences in my childhood, overall, I saw more poverty mindset, depression, struggle, stagnancy, insecurity, drug and alcohol influence, and unstable parenting than anything else. Still, in my childhood years, I decided that those curses would not follow me into my adulthood. I decided that my children would be created for signs and wonders immediately upon conception and everything in my life nourished that thought process. Because Everything initiates in the mind, my first assignment was to protect my thoughts. I only wanted to allow positive, progressive, and joyful thoughts to be a part of this growth journey, and my goal was to continue that throughout their lives. There are some simple practices and affirmations to see this through.

1. Only allow positive energy in your space- that doesn't mean that you will never encounter negativity, but it does mean that it's your responsibility to remove it or remove yourself from it.

2. The law of attraction is real- you attract what you think/are. So, if you change your thinking, you change your life. This, in essence, will Automatically keep the negativity at bay.

3. Read- read to yourself, which will transfer to reading to your unborn child. Don't just read Children's books. Read self-help, financial freedom, and other books about winning for you and your baby.

4. Laugh a lot.

5. Breastfeed, if at all possible, for at least a year or as long as you possibly can. (Benefits of Breastfeeding - Capital Women's Care | MD, DC, & VA, n.d.) "Breast milk provides abundant and easily absorbed nutritional components, antioxidants, enzymes, immune properties, and live antibodies from the mother. Mother's more mature immune system makes antibodies to the germs to which she and her baby have been exposed. These antibodies enter her milk to help protect her baby from illness. Immunoglobulin A coats the lining of the baby's

immature intestines helping germs and allergens from leaking through. Breast milk also contains substances that naturally soothe infants.)

I breastfed both of my babies. I didn't mention it yet, but they are only 12 months and 8 days apart. It felt like raising twins, and for a short time, both of them wanted to be on the breast. My son was first, and it was challenging in the beginning, but I took lactation classes and pushed through mastitis (Benefits of Breastfeeding - Capital Women's Care | MD, DC, & VA, n.d.) (An inflammation of breast tissue that sometimes involves an infection. The inflammation results in breast pain, swelling, warmth, and redness. You may also have a fever and chills. This is usually caused by blocked milk ducts.) After a couple of months, it was smooth sailing and worth every challenge. The biggest gift was and still is the bond. Nursing creates a bond like no other, and you are literally transferring energy at every feeding. When my daughter was born, it was a similar but unique experience, and I was more seasoned. I had it down to a science, learned how to pump as I feed and store my milk, and it hindered nothing in my life. My children definitely gained all of the benefits above, and they have been brilliant since infancy.

6. Take classes and get as much guidance as possible on labor and delivery and figure out the safest space for you to have a successful, stress-free delivery.

7. Prepare the space where your baby will sleep and thrive. Don't wait until just before the due date. If you feel rushed, your baby feels that anxiety. Do all the fun stuff and take the time to plan colors and themes that resonate with the desire of your baby. If that includes a gender

reveal or a baby shower, do whatever makes you feel good. Remember, our subconscious mind needs to be conditioned to think grand and expect whatever we desire. A great time to start teaching this mindset is in the womb. The baby's energy is already transferring and manifesting.

8. AND make sure the outside environment, including the people involved, is as perfect as possible when your bundle of joy arrives!

Everything that I'm writing, I practiced as a young Mom. I led by example, and I practiced what I preached. It's important to allow your children to develop and unapologetically be themselves. If their environment is conducive to greatness, you won't have to do much punishing. Redirecting will satisfy most of the corrections needed at that age. I am aware that children not only follow the example of their parents but anything else that they are able to observe, which is why a controlled environment makes the learning process flow more smoothly. Michigan State University did an article on March 30, 2015, about children being observational learners that speaks to the point that I'm making. (Miller, 2022) "Children learn from models all around them, on television, in the grocery store, at school, and at home.

You have likely witnessed some observational learning with your child or even in your interactions with other children. Maybe your child comes home from school casting imaginary webs like Spiderman, even though they have never had any introduction to the character at home. Or perhaps they show off a new, not-so-child-friendly vocabulary word after the family reunion. Wherever they are, whoever they are around, children are observing and learning.

Watching a specific behavior does not necessarily mean a child will perform the behavior themselves; watching someone break a toy does not automatically mean your child will begin destroying things. Whether or not they demonstrate a new behavior, they are picking up new knowledge. Children are learning about the behavioral choices of others and also about the consequences of those behaviors.

What modeled behaviors children will imitate depends partly on what sort of reinforcement those behaviors receive. People are more likely to imitate a behavior if they get some sort of positive reinforcement for it. For example, if a child overhears another child swearing, he might learn new words but may not necessarily use them. If, however, the child gets some sort of reward for swearing, such as acceptance or encouragement from an adult, an observing child might be more likely to copy this behavior. Don't forget that laughter can be an unintended positive reinforcement. The same can be said if someone witnesses a negative reinforcement, such as scolding for swearing. A child may be less likely to imitate the behavior.

Through the process of modeling, children can learn aggressive behaviors by observing them. Sometimes this occurs through live models and direct experiences, but it often happens by watching television and other programs where aggressive behaviors occur. If these aggressive behaviors are reinforced, children might be likely to imitate them and execute aggressive acts themselves.

On the opposite end of the spectrum, children can also acquire prosocial behaviors through observational learning. Watching someone cooperate, share, take turns, and demonstrate altruistic acts can teach children to show those behaviors too."

In the Universe and when it comes to attraction, positive thinking heavily outweighs negative thinking, so in order to combat constantly battling negative outside forces, put your children in positive outside environments as often as possible. Being a mommypreneur made this effortless. If I was around greatness, so were my kids. I didn't keep them away from my businesses; instead, I included them in the business environment. They were around wealth and prosperity. They were around positive, progressive conversations that included plans for success. They were constantly in environments that displayed our family winning and going to the next level. It automatically taught their subconscious mind that winning was not only normal, but it was the only way. I explained to them what I was doing if there was an insurance or investment presentation taking place, and I fed into the inquisitive angle of their little minds figuring it out.

It was also important for them to be well-traveled at a young age. I'm not saying that you must go to Bali when your kids are 4 but at least allow them to see beyond their usual location. This trains their subconscious mind as well, and their ego doesn't have to rescue them from future adventures and opportunities due to the fear of the unknown. Disney world doesn't just have to be on T.V. Take them places and let them touch things that would otherwise seem impossible.

Growing up, I didn't know that most of what I saw others doing on T.V. was attainable because I only experienced traveling distances no more than 40- 50 miles my entire childhood. Don't get me wrong, that bubble was full of fun times and fond memories, but it also brought limitations, walls, and boxes. I'm forever grateful for the meeting that helped me change my subconscious mind and my willingness to follow. There are many success stories about people figuring it out despite their upbringing. This book, however, is just my suggestions on how to make that pavement smoother from the beginning for your children. Once this foundation is solid, they will have better footing as you unleash them into this huge world.

Chapter 9
Let's go to school

U nless they are homeschooled, your child will spend just as much time at school as they do at home on any given weekday. This makes being intentional about their educational choices mandatory. They will likely be shaped and influenced by their educational experiences just as much, if not more than they will in their family environment. I have many experiences to tell you about school, but I will narrow it down for the sake of the book. My children were taught in hand-picked private school environments except for the year that we were transitioning from one city to another. I know someone is saying, "How do you expect me to pay for a hand-picked private school?" Remember, the Universe will release to you whatever you truly believe you deserve. If I gave you my tax documents in 2007 and beyond, you would absolutely wonder how I successfully put my kids through private school for most of their life. However, If I let you into my brain for the same time period, you would see that it was destined, expected, and manifested. If you are willing, I can teach you to do the same.

Remember the boat in the flood? You just need to make sure that you don't miss the boat. And the beautiful thing about the Universe is, if you fail forward, the boat usually comes back around again. There are usually scholarships, financial aid, and other provisions that keep income from being the sole purpose of denial into most schools. You have to do your due diligence, and you have to have a sense of urgency doing it but remember, belief is always the first step to any manifestation.

So now I'll tell you about one of the staples of my children's lives. We were looking for a school, and of course, I put the energy in Universe, and the Universe did the rest. I was at an insurance meeting the week after choosing the area for the school, and I met a lady. She just happened to be explaining her children's new potential private school, and she said they were looking for minority students. She pulled up the school online, and as soon as I saw the campus, it resonated with my spirit. I immediately wrote down the information and shared it with my children when the workday was done. They were equally excited, and we called the school the next morning. The school obviously had an open appointment for the very next day, so we locked it in and talked about our expectations for most of the evening.

We woke up the next morning and made the 45 min drive to the school. When we arrived, it was even more exhilarating than the website. "This looks like camp," Vj said, and Micah agreed. This is the description directly from the website…. (Peele, 2022) "Woodlawn's 61-acre wooded campus provides a unique, almost pastoral atmosphere that enhances students' learning experiences. The southeastern quarter of the campus contains the historic 1836 Woodlawn home, as well as two of the home's outbuildings that were renovated in 2002 to form the first classroom buildings. Two additional classroom buildings were built over the next three years. In 2007, our first capital campaign led to the construction of an

Upper School building and a gymnasium. In 2010, a second campaign allowed us to build a classroom building and a Lodge used for classes and events. A barn built in 1910 still stands on the eastern edge of the campus, while the remainder of the property is forested, with a small stream flowing east toward the Rocky River."

If you can picture that description, take away nothing and add love; you have just arrived at Woodlawn School in August of 2011. We walked through the doors of Woodlawn Home and were warmly greeted and welcomed. We toured the school and listened to the structure of the curriculum as well as the freedom of accepting the Woodlawn honor code and allowing the growth to manifest. The students were expected to do nothing more than be themselves and attract greatness. There was no dress code, no crazy rules, and no boring daily classroom, only learning. The 5-figure admission cost was no deterrent in our excitement because if The Most High led us to it, He would definitely see us through it. And it wasn't something that we wanted; it was something that had just manifested in our life. In other words, it was already done.

I'm not sure who was more excited, me or the kids. They had an interactive curriculum; for example, if they were studying the Renaissance in History, they were also studying it in English, Art, Science, etc. It was a well-oiled machine, and each class connected the dots. Oh, I forgot to tell you that the school had just over 100 students k-12 when we started, meaning no class was far over double digits, if that. Many days class was on the lawn and consisted more of a hands-on project or experience versus bookwork. They were taught in a way that made them understand the subject matter and not just learn how to pass a test. I remember VJ coming home one day and explaining fractions to me. I'm a little embarrassed to say that I was a former 8th grade math teacher, and my 4th grader broke down what fractions were and how to solve them in a way that I hadn't learned or understood in high school or college! By 5th grade,

Micah could write a dissertation better than most of my friends in graduate school. We would cook and frequently include the herbs that were cultivated by the kids in their Woodlawn Garden. Every year there was a different service-learning project assigned by grade level, and one that was very memorable was Micah's 3rd grade location. They had to volunteer at the Mooresville Women's shelter. Micah has always been a Mama Bear and loves helping less fortunate people feel better. She's always been the advocate for the underdog, and she is unapologetic about her stance of treating people kindly. She was beyond shocked when she first realized that these mothers with children were homeless and hungry. She took so much pride in not just passing out food but talking to the kids and making artwork to brighten up the shelter. It put our gratitude in perspective, and it was one of those moments that she realized we were different. Not because we weren't homeless but because we believed and expected greatness subconsciously, so this was not even a thought in her conscious mind. This experience was among so many; I could go on for many chapters. Woodlawn did not steer the students in any direction but instead encouraged individuality and concentration on each individual purpose they had in this life. The mission is to produce independent, lifelong learners who are responsible, contributing members of a diverse global society. This mission rings true for my 2 and many of their peers that came through with them.

Chapter 10
Activities

Live intentionally! You're in control of your destiny.
It's merely the manifestations of what
you've chosen to accept or deny.
Autrina

My children have been participating in extracurricular activities consistently since they were old enough to join. I never pushed them in any direction, but I did pay attention to their obvious gifts and personality traits in order to encourage and cultivate any interest in that direction. They were kids, so they didn't always stick to the plan; however, I taught them every principle that I talked about in this book. I taught it by example and reiterated it through instruction. Every moment was a teachable moment in our world. I have always been the 'don't sweat the small stuff,' let's focus on the solution, not the problem, and we can accomplish absolutely anything that we desire type of mom. I have been unwavering in my intentional living outlook since before they could talk. This was not too much or too hard for them. It was normal because that's all they knew. It's still all they know, and anyone that knows us will attest that we have a ball being extraordinary. I didn't differentiate the magnitude of the principles according to their age, just the method by which I conveyed them.

A principle is a fundamental truth or proposition that serves as the foundation for a system of belief or behavior or for a chain of reasoning. They had the freedom to choose, but they learned that

> practice makes permanent, and only perfect practice
> makes perfect. You have to practice how to
> think correctly and how to react….
> They learned to work.

> Do what most people won't do so you can
> have what most people won't have.

> Success is a quality decision backed up by commitment,
> and you must choose every day.

> Consistency- you must get frequent before you get great.

> We create our existence…Feeling vs. Doing. Feelers
> act when they feel like it. Doers act
> their way into feeling

> Gratitude is appreciating what you have as opposed to what
> you want. Don't get stuck in the process of wanting
> but instead continues to attract and manifest
> what you desire in present tense
> and practice gratitude
> without ceasing.

> Roots create the fruits….to change the visible, you must
> first change the invisible. If your current fruit
> is rotten, it's ok; that's in the past.
> Time for a new harvest.

These are just a few of the principles that I consistently practiced and preached, and they subconsciously took them into every adventure in their life.

Chapter 11
My Young King

Michael is of Hebrew origin, and it means "who is like God?" He came into this world in the full magnitude of just that, and his presence continues to be loud and Supernatural. Because we can manifest what we desire, I decided immediately that I would have a daughter shortly after, and she would be called Micah, which also translates to "who is like God?" 12 months later, that desire was realized, and you will read about her later.

Michael quickly adopted several nicknames, including VJ (the most common for him growing up), Nuke (his paternal grandparents did that), and Puna (My nickname that, unfortunately for him, I still call him to this day). He has always been very determined and passionate about winning and having fun doing it. He started walking at 6 months old, and he's been on the move ever since. He has had an extreme amount of integrity, confidence, and ambition since I can remember. He has always been academically gifted and athletically talented, so we'll start with his lifelong journey in baseball.

Baseball Mom is what they call me. We started with Tee ball as soon as he was old enough to play, and I remember him carrying that tee around to grandpa's house or wherever he was going to be able to practice. Practice makes permanent and perfect practice makes perfect were principles that he adopted and continued throughout his childhood. We started with Rec Ball, and he played every season, matriculating to each level his age. When he was about 8 years old, he started playing for the Braves, and he was very fast. He earned the nickname Jackie from all the coaches and even started wearing a jersey with the number 42. He would hit the ball and run to 1st base, then proceed to put on a show. Everyone would wait in anticipation as his coaches would instruct him to steal every base. The other teams knew what was about to happen, but his timing and speed couldn't be stopped. He could beat 'em in a pickle (A rundown- a situation that occurs when the baserunner is stranded between two bases, also known as no man's land, and is in jeopardy of being tagged out), slide underneath the glove of each infielder or just simply outrun whoever was chasing him. He played Rec ball until it was no longer challenging, and then we decided to switch to travel ball. This was a big change and required even more commitment, but he was fit for the challenge. We traveled for over a year with one team but decided to move on to his final baseball home around the age of 13/14.

Team Carolina was pivotal and manifested for many reasons beyond baseball. We were doing some extra training at a baseball facility (Michael was always doing extra training), and one of the training coaches referred us to Coach Maddox. He was the founder and head coach, and he created an environment where kids had the chance to maximize their potential in baseball as well as in life. I believe wholeheartedly in mentorship, and if you are a single mother or you just want to breed powerful, meaningful environments for your children, sports can be a great choice. Of course, you want to speak positive affirmations and pray your prayers of gratitude continuously as you collaborate with the Universe to manifest the perfect destination. Because Michael's energy demanded greatness, all his coaches impacted his life in one way or another. Sometimes I would walk into Coach Maddox's office and expect a baseball conversation, but instead, I would encounter a manhood conversation as he taught the boys lessons to live by. His tough love and genuine concern for those who valued themselves balanced many decisions and situations throughout our tenure with Team Carolina.

Baseball Mom has to be one of my favorite motherhood adventures. We traveled from city to city and state to state season after season. We developed bonds that would impact us forever, including frequently being in hotel rooms with my children and working as a team to make sure everything ran smoothly. Me and my 2 have always been ride or die, and I can't type this without tears falling on the keys of my laptop. We sang songs on the road like in the movies, we ate so much food, and we maximized whatever location we traveled to. It was our goal to visit the attractions, beaches, and whatever that city is famous for. Did it cost a lot? Well, that's all relative, but you already know that I'm going to tell you that the Universe had that handled. We just speak what we desire and pray prayers of gratitude that we have it, and Manifestation is inevitable. Maybe if I say this enough, you'll start to believe me. I was a single mom working for myself, and my bank account did not support everything that we accomplished, but The Most High, Yah, did!

Michael also met his best friends during our stint with Team Carolina, and I'm sure those bonds will last a lifetime. They have become brothers and partners in greatness, and I gained more sons that I love dearly.

He also played soccer and basketball throughout his middle school and high school years. He was just good at everything. Michael is gifted and athletic, but even more than that, he is an extremely hard worker and proud of his accomplishments. Hard work beats skill any day of the week.

I took pride in dressing my children ever since they were babies. They both could have been Gap brand ambassadors, just to name one of my clothing store obsessions. They were on point every time, and you were not going to catch me off my game when it came to my polished babies! They developed their own style as they grew, but it still mirrored the energy I put into them their whole childhood. Around the age of 14, Michael was attempting to dress up to go to an event, and he wanted to buy a french cuff cutaway collar shirt. We searched every store you could think of, including online, and soon realized that this shirt did not exist for boys and teens. They were only available in men's sizes. Well, since my children's subconscious minds have been conditioned to create whatever they desire, Michael's immediate idea was just to create his own. He came to me and inquired how he could design his own shirt for boys and sell it. Surely, he wasn't the only young man who wanted to look dapper at a formal event. Of course, my immediate answer was absolutely, and although I had no idea what to do first, I put it in the Universe and started researching with Michael.

I can't make this stuff up, but about 2 weeks later, a friend I had briefly shared Michael's idea with called. He said that one of his friends has a male clothing business that is shutting down, and he's looking for a way to wholesale about 100 suits and even more dress shirts and men's accessories. I went to the warehouse and called Michael, who was visiting his grandparents at the time. I took a picture of the suits, sent it to him, and asked him if he was ready to start the business he had asked me about. I could hear the elation through the phone! "Mommy," he said, "are you serious right now?!" "Yes, sir," I said back to him. It was on! I bought all the inventory for little to nothing, and Michael came home to get to work. We bought clothing racks and organized everything in the loft at our home. Classic Man would be the name of the business, and Michael came up with every idea himself. We contacted an artist to create the logo, ordered business cards, got an EIN number, created the LLC, and opened a bank account all within 14 days' time.

Michael's passion for starting Classic Man was to give boys the opportunity to dress just as stylishly as men, so although we had mostly men's sizes currently, he set out to design his French cuff, cutaway collar shirt for boys. We sent the design idea to a manufacturer in China and bought samples until it was just right. We ordered his design in boys' sizes 4 to 18 and continued to plan ideas for the launch of Classic Man LLC. Word spread]fast of course, because energy is neither created nor destroyed but transferred from one source to another. We got a call from another fellow entrepreneur that heard about the development of Classic Man and invited Michael to participate in the Charlotte Small Business Expo one month later. He was 14 yall! Michael didn't skip a beat, and now we had to order banners, signs, payment-accepting equipment, receipt books, etc.

"Done is better than perfect."
Sheryl Sandberg

That experience and exposure were second to none, and watching my young king interview and present himself with poise and confidence made mommying worth every late night and every sacrifice. He didn't stop there, and next, we began to promote fashion shows. His name and his mission were being shared, and he was invited to style and organize the look of the participants of several fashion shows. Classic man attire was the exclusive brand for the young men in the shows, and Michael walked around with his tape measure and eye of intention to ensure that everything looked as he envisioned it. He has been blessed to have more than just mommy in his corner. There have been more people than I would even attempt to mention looking out and making ways for him to carry out his many aspirations so far.

Well, I guess I should wrap this up and bring you up to speed on current times. I could talk about the journey with my children for days, but this book is supposed to be just enough to inspire mommypreneurs. During Michael's senior year in high school, he decided that he'd received everything he was purposed to receive in baseball. He wanted to focus on being an entrepreneur and getting wealthy. All he talked about was starting companies and trading stock and cryptocurrency. He applied to a few colleges but had his heart set on either Elon University or North Carolina State University due to their extensive programs in Entrepreneurial studies. We visited both and even had an opportunity to meet the dean of Entrepreneurship and attend a class at Elon. The meeting was fascinating, and I'm not sure who was more excited afterward; Michael or me.

He applied to both schools, and of course, he was accepted. In addition, he received a full academic scholarship at Elon and was honored as an Odyssey Scholar. Elon is a smaller University with an intimate campus, and he was used to having a close relationship with his teachers, so we thought this would fit him perfectly. He is a Boss in every fiber of his body, so school, although a great accomplishment, has had to be put in perspective a few times since he started. He is now a junior and thinking of new endeavors daily as the last two years of college play out. About a year ago, he decided that he wanted to join My fiancé and I in the real estate field, and if you are my child, "thoughts become things." He is now a realtor with Armstrong Realty Group, and of course, he has hit the ground running. The sky is not the limit because there are no limitations, and as long as I am present in this lifetime, I am here for every twist and turn.

Created for signs and wonders

By design, you are a King

When you walk, the ground opens up

And the Universe thinks

Of ways to grant more favor

What flavors of greatness are great enough

For your youthful desires

Though not yet, Manhood is swiftly upon you

But the masses presently inspired

Your eyes glow, your ears yearn,

Your soul gives, and your heart burns

Your spirit prays without ceasing

Your purpose is intentional, intentionally

Wonderfully and fearfully made!

You are my breath, you are my heartbeat, you are my smile, you are my tears

You are my SON.

And my love is eternally unconditional!

Chapter 12
My Goddess in the Making

Micah has always been my artist. She started talking and singing before age 1 and was speaking in clear, concise, grammatically correct sentences by 18 months old. Singing, dancing, playing instruments, and acting were all right up her alley. I saw early on that artistry was her thing, so even though she went back and forth in her activity decisions, I encouraged anything that involved artistry. Sometimes we make extracurricular activities stressful for our kids. There is a way to take the path of least resistance by letting them choose but suggesting and guiding them in their area of interest. Praise and gratitude are huge, and you must do this continuously to mold their subconscious minds. Micah started out at six years old doing competition cheerleading. Her team was the Stars, and she tumbled and yelled her way to excitement during every practice and competition. Every part of cheering didn't come naturally to her, but her determination and belief that she could do anything yielded success every time. We would get on the road and travel to the cheer competitions. The girls were hyper and prissy, putting on makeup with their big red hairbows and their red, white, and blue cheer uniforms. They worked hard, and the moms worked harder. The competitions were long and exciting, and the experience was worth the preparation and sacrifice.

I remember taking Micah to her first acting audition around the same age. The initial instructions were to stand at the front with your headshot, introduce yourself and tell us what you want to be when you grow up. All of the beautiful children stood in front and held their photos as they professed to become doctors, lawyers, firemen, police officers, and teachers. Micah trotted to the front when it was her turn. With the biggest smile I've ever seen, she loudly and clearly pronounced her full name and age. Then she did a little two-step and yelled, "I'm going to be a Hollywood Superstar!" She stole the show as usual, and my friends that were there still talk about it to this day.

Another activity that was constant for quite a while was the Charlotte Children's theater program. I'll take a break again to talk about my ability, mostly as a single mother, to afford and make time for activities. We spoke it, attracted it, manifested it, and the Universe did the rest. It's really that simple, and if you need help learning, our coaching program is just a phone call or an email away. One rule of thumb is to get in early. Most programs have scholarships, aid, early registration discounts, etc. The way is already made; you just have to believe. The performance that I remember most was a musical entitled Bye Bye Birdie. She looked like she'd been doing it for years. Afterward, all her supporters were waiting with flowers, gifts, and an abundance of praise.

Micah has done so much; dance, piano, guitar, vocals, musicals, writing, and just about any form of artistry you can fathom. It's in her soul, and it is a great part of her existence. Two of the last big things she participated in before college were a program with her vocal instructor, Jason Jett, and a prestigious summer camp at Berklee College of Music. Young Icons was and is still a phenomenal program for young musically inclined and artistically gifted youth.

It is a Multi-week intensive summer camp. They put kids in real studios and guide them every step of the way in making a hit song. Micah made her first professional track titled "King Kong," and it was amazing. Jason not only cultivated this successful program, but he has been one of the instrumental mentors in Micah's success throughout high school and entering college. Micah has always been a natural, but with age, she has become more of a perfectionist and a little more timid at times. Jason patiently helped her master her craft over the course of about 4 years.

Berklee was another adventure. "Mommy, there's this program that I want to apply for, and it's in Boston," said Micah. It was the summer before her sophomore year at Woodlawn, and she was deep in her music. Berklee had an intensive summer camp that was designed to enhance your skills and allow you to apply new influences to your craft while learning from renowned faculty and visiting artists. She applied, was accepted and we set sail for greatness, just me and my princess. We had so much fun, and watching her newfound independence was inspiring. We flew to Boston, Ma, and got settled in our hotel room. One of Micah's classmates also attended the summer camp, so we met up with her family on the first day as we made our way to the auditorium to register. Micah joined her group and didn't waste any time as they immediately had to start an assignment creating an individual act to perform in front of an audience. It was an amazing experience, and of course, my baby was a shining star! She gained so much knowledge and exposure not only at the camp but also exploring Boston. For the first time ever, we rode the train and a city bus together on our mommy/daughter excursions. We shopped, and of course, we ate as we discovered Boston. She met new friends in the program from other states and even other countries. It was cute when she figured out ways to ditch me because she wanted some peer time. I loved it, and of course, I figured out how to explore solo during those times. Another memory and another experience in the books for her to take into her future success.

Jason helped with the Berklee audition as well as exposure in a 2nd Young Icon program, and by senior year she was well on her way to the next level. Still very supportive, he along with her latest music mentor Serena held her hand through auditions and applications that landed her a music scholarship at Loyola University in New Orleans, Louisiana.

The Law of Attraction was in action again! Micah had applied to several schools just for formality, but she had a few top choices, and she actually got accepted and awarded scholarships for those schools. We only had to visit two schools because Loyola was the 2nd one, and she immediately said, "Yes to the College." Of course, all of the hard work and belief paid off. Loyola has a state-of-the-art music program and is the home of many professional movie and music productions. As we toured the campus and specifically the Music building, she fit right in. She was so excited; it felt like the day that she proclaimed her stardom in Hollywood at 6 years old. It all fell into place, and she was soon moving into her dorm. I couldn't believe my baby was in college. She met friends and associates, and I trusted that everything I taught her would shine through whenever needed. She participates in an ensemble that performs twice a year at a local club in New Orleans. The first performance was a few months after school started; we packed up and flew down to see what all the hype was about, and she didn't disappoint. The next semester she performed at the same location, Tipitinas, New Orleans. About a month before the performance, she told me that she would be singing one of my favorite songs, 'The Way by Jill Scott.' She practiced a lot, but this song was in her natural voice range and style, so I knew she would kill it! She told me that I may get to sing it with her, but unfortunately, she could only do it with her band. This was a class assignment but make no doubt about it; it was a real club atmosphere and event. This time she had an entourage. Between family and friends, she had at least 10 out-of-town supporters, and she made sure to put on a show. Even as a freshman, she made it Micah's show, and she had the crowd in an uproar. Of course, I was the loudest and as close to the stage as possible; I was so proud of my baby girl.

It's easy to shine when everything is smooth sailing, but I'm most proud of her ability to handle adversity. She hit a few freshman bumps during her first year and didn't wait for Mommy to fix them. She made some decisions and expected the Universe to come through. She persevered and didn't show an ounce of worry as she demanded her outcome and manifested ease. This is when a proud moment becomes an unforgettable moment and magnifies my attitude of gratitude. I now have a sophomore at Loyola University, and she ceases to amaze me continuously. I'm one proud mom, and this journey just gets better and better.

A few important things to tell your daughter:

- Always wear clean, intact underwear…. In case you're in an accident, and they have to cut your clothes off.
- It's ok to cry, even when you're hurt, angry or sad. But you got 5 min; wash your face, clean up your mess and get up off the floor when you're done. You don't belong there. You were created for signs and wonders, and you're destined for greatness.
- Seek out people and places that resonate with your frequency.
- Just because you can, doesn't mean you should
- Can't never could. We only speak prosperity into the Universe.
- Your body, your rules.
- Just do it, fail forward, fail big and keep collaborating with the Universe to manifest every desire.

- Say please, thank you, and excuse me whenever the situation warrants them.
- Never say, "I'm sorry." I apologize is efficient.
- You are connected to the source, so you have enough. You are enough.
- You are amazing! Don't ever let anyone make you feel that you aren't. If someone attempts to, simply walk away. You deserve better.
- Be happy and stay true to your roots because they run deep and strong.
- Say what you mean and mean what you say.
- No one will ever love you more than I do.
- When in doubt, remember whose daughter you are and straighten your crown!!!

Chapter 13
Mommypreneur

You can make excuses, or you can create a legacy,
but you can't do both.
Autrina

I had just finished breastfeeding 2 babies 2 years back-to-back when I started my first entrepreneurial journey. Mommying was my most cherished assignment, and I asked the Universe daily to show me how to manifest a legacy for my heartbeats. When I was introduced to that couple making the $250k, I knew it wasn't by accident, and I didn't need another sign to get going. It took me about 6 months to prepare myself, and from that point forward, in 2004, I have been in control of my income. I was immediately surrounded by greatness, and I soaked it all up. I quickly obtained my life/health insurance license, and I learned how to educate families in insurance literacy. I taught myself as I taught others how to determine their financial needs by first doing an analysis. I was a straight-A student from kindergarten till 12th grade and I had a college degree with a double major in biology and chemistry; however, I had never been taught anything about money or finance. I quickly learned that the educational system was designed strategically, and if you want to be wealthy, it is up to you and your family.

I learned that insurance is the foundation of any financial plan and why fish frys and the jar at the convenient store to raise money for a funeral was birthed from a poverty mentality. I learned that insurance was the easiest way to leave an inheritance and create a legacy, and it could also be used as a living benefit. I learned about using insurance as a tax shelter and how wealthy people use life insurance to pay estate taxes on a large inheritance. I also learned why most of our grandparents paid for a life insurance policy for most of their lives, but when they passed away, we still barely have enough insurance money to bury them. This is where knowledge of the different types of life insurance is crucial. Melanated people associated life insurance with death, not wealth, and this ignorance is one of the lingering effects of our PTSD from being enslaved. I learned that term, whole life, group, universal life, and variable universal life all have their place, and if you don't have expert knowledge or guidance, you will likely lose every time.

I strive to teach insurance literacy to everyone that will allow me into their space. It is a part of my purpose, and I understood that very quickly. Insurance, coupled with saving and being mentored and guided in every aspect of money, will lead to financial freedom and change the outline of generations to come.

Another fascinating concept I learned early on what the "rule of 72."

It is a simple way to determine how long an investment will take to double, given a fixed annual rate of interest. By dividing 72 by the annual rate of return, investors obtain a rough estimate of how many years it will take for the initial investment to duplicate itself. For example: If you invested $5,000 in your savings account, giving you a 1% return, it would take 72 years for it to double to 10,000. That same $5000 in an investment vehicle averaging a 12% return would double in just 6 years. Why had nobody told me this before?

Another calculation using this compound interest concept is: If you start saving $500/month at age 25, you'll have $2,073,982 by retirement age at 67. That same $500/month starting at age 40 will yield $574,000 by retirement at 67. Now, of course, if you want to retire sooner, you just need to save more, but these examples allow you to look at saving in a whole new light. This should be the conversation at the dinner table. However, even if you have knowledge of these concepts, unless you have a wealthy mentality and the discipline to put them into action, it's just numbers on paper. I wasn't in position early on, nor was I aware of these concepts, but to be able to start my children on the right path from scratch is changing the generational future of my family tree.

While we are on a roll, I'll tell you about one more lesson I learned early on studying financial freedom. The cash flow quadrant changed everything I thought I knew about making money. There are 4 ways, and if you earn money, you fall into one of these categories. In Robert Kyosaki's book "Rich Dad's Cash Flow Quadrant," he reveals how some people work less, earn more, pay less in taxes, and learn to become financially free. (Invest in Real Estate. Do What Matters., 2022) The 4 ways to earn income are as an:

E – Employee

An employee has a job. This is where most people earn their income. The job itself is owned by a business, which could be a single person or a large corporation. The employee trades his or her time, energy, and skills to an employer in exchange for a paycheck and benefits.

Employees can make a little or a lot of money. But when if an employee closes the business, downsizes, or just decides that they no longer need you in that position, your income stops also.

This long-term lack of control over income is the primary problem of the E quadrant. An employee's financial destiny, security, and freedom are dependent upon the decisions and the success of their employer.

S – Self-Employed

Many employees get tired of their lack of control and decide to work for themselves. The self-employed still work, but they own their job.

The S quadrant includes dentists, insurance agents, restaurant owners, realtors, handymen, and many other trade workers. Many self-employed people earn very large incomes, but like the employee, when they stop working, so does their income. There's not much room for sick days or long vacations.

Self-employed people do have a lot more control than an employee, but that also means they have more responsibility. As a result, success usually means working harder and working longer. After a long period of time, this can lead to burnout and fatigue.

If you have a plan in place, however, you can transition your self-employment journey to building a business. Mentorship is a great way to do this faster.

B – Business Owner

Those in the B quadrant own a system and lead people. The systems and people who work for the business can run successfully without the business owner's constant involvement.

The same types of businesses could be run by S owners and B owners. For example, a plumber could own and work in his own plumbing business, or a business owner could create a plumbing business and hire quality plumbers, administrators, and a manager to run the systems of the plumbing business. An insurance broker could hire other agents to work with the customers, and a real estate broker can do the same. You can even start a lawn care service and hire workers to maintain the yard of your clients.

The wealthiest individuals in the world typically own businesses. These include Bill Gates of Microsoft, Jeff Bezos of Amazon, and Mark Zuckerberg of Facebook.

I – Investors

Investors own assets that produce income. This is the quadrant for truly passive income.

Investors in this quadrant have usually accumulated money earned in one or more of the other three quadrants, and they let the money go to work and produce even more money for themselves.

Investors often purchase shares of companies owned by those in the B quadrant. The capital from the investors helps to fuel the systems created by the business owner, and this fuel can lead to even greater growth (and more income) for everyone involved.

Investors can also use their money to buy real estate and other currency that gives immediate returns and returns much higher than the examples in the rule of 72. Most smart business owners are also investors and have money working for them in many different ways.

There are multiple paths to <u>financial independence</u>, but most of them ultimately lead to the right side of the quadrant – B and I. So, if you want to achieve greater financial independence and freedom, it will pay to start learning the skills and mindset required to make this move to the right side.

These concepts had me locked in at the tender age of 26. I decided to share this knowledge with as many people as possible. I had a desire to enlighten more people with a similar story as mine and also to move through the quadrants as quickly as possible. I read books like "Secrets of a Millionaire Mind," "How to Win Friends and Influence People," "Developing the Leader Within You," "Developing the Leaders Around You," and many more. I was hungry for knowledge and determined to win! I learned the most successful 1% of great leaders all mastered acquiring and keeping good people around them. You must develop the leaders around you because the strength of an organization is the direct result of the strength of its leaders.

So now, not only was I focused on learning everything there was to know about insurance and financial freedom, but I was also focused on building. I learned how to organize and host seminars and opportunity meetings. I learned how to prospect and relate to people as I taught them how to gain the same knowledge I was gaining. I learned how to train agents on content as well as leadership, and I quickly became a leader and top producer in the company. Although I was self-employed, I was well on my way to becoming a business owner. I was doing six-figure production personally and much more with my team. I spoke in front of hundreds and eventually thousands of people, putting in 12+ hour workdays on a regular basis. I drove 100k miles every year for several years, building my business. I helped countless numbers of families and agents alike, and you must be asking yourself, how did you do this as a mom? The short answer is my kids did it with me. I worked many hours, but I still controlled my time. My children were at most meetings and many individual appointments. My children could probably do a presentation better than most new agents by the age of 6. They were around millionaires and at conferences in California before they were in kindergarten. They screamed positive affirmations and prayed gratitude prayers with me before they even fully understood them. But they just knew that it felt good, Mommy was a Boss, and their subconscious minds were being fed with expectations of greatness! I knew that the countless hours wouldn't last long if I made them count. I knew that by the time the age of extracurricular activities and school functions started, I would be able to let my business work for me. There was a method to my madness. You ask, were there hard days, tears, critical decisions, missed client appointments, not tucking the kids in a few times a month, failing forward, choosing to invest in a business advancement instead of buying a personal item? Absolutely, but you can choose to make excuses, or you can create a legacy; you can't do both. This insurance and financial literacy journey was a manifestation of my prayers of gratitude, and my determination to cultivate my mental fortitude made all the difference in my endurance. Building a business is not for the faint at heart, but the rewards far outweigh the risks. Mindset remains the most important part of any achievement. If you believe it, you can achieve it, but if not, you can work until your brain bleeds, and you will never make it beyond lack.

Chapter 14
Adding legs to my craft

Eventually, I received everything that I needed from my current business environment, and I decided to jump again. I started another insurance company without the backing of a large corporation and learned how to cut out most of the middle. I created my own vision and even bigger goals. I had learned so much and became an expert in the field, and this made me hungry to offer my clients more. I ventured deep into the health insurance market to learn that many people in the low to middle income class also didn't understand or have sufficient health insurance. I mastered Medicare insurance and carried my seminar skills over to that market. I continued to do life insurance and financial literacy seminars adding things like; how to avoid senior scams and how understanding Medicare Parts A, B, C, and D.

My seminars were rewarding, and I continued to add certifications and licenses to my resume to be a one-stop shop for my clients. I also continued mindset training and self-improvement by reading books, going to conferences, and listening to leaders and mentors. The Universe continued to put me on the path of everything I needed to fulfill everything I spoke. I met a couple of agents that were also experts in the tax and accounting field, and I learned even more about how insurance and taxes coincided. It helped me greatly once the affordable care act came into play, and I was able to better assist my clients that were business owners as well refer them to my friends for accounting services. Many entrepreneurs are not efficiently insured because they just don't know how to take advantage of all the perks and benefits offered by the government. Many families have been living for years practicing pay-as-you-go health insurance. This is not cost-effective and lacks the ability to satisfy all your healthcare needs. Most people have no idea what the health insurance subsidy really is or how it's just a tax credit that you are able to use to pay your health insurance premium. Most people just dial a 1-800 number and let the person on the other end of the phone sign them up for whatever they say is best. If you ask them to explain what just happened, they can explain it about as well each prescription they take. My mission is to encourage people to understand what they have instead of just buying what sounds good. Don't get me wrong, it can still sound good and be good, but that doesn't mean that you shouldn't want clarity. When you are unclear, you will not maximize the benefit of whatever you are doing.

My insurance business was booming, and I had been in business for some time when I met a handsome guy in the line at Best Buy, and we exchanged business cards. Davis Armstrong Jr., Armstrong Realty Group, is what was displayed on the card. I wasn't interested, however, in the Real Estate business until years later when I not only became his business partner but his fiancé. Our story is another book, but when we started dating, I had the pleasure of tagging along to view houses for potential clients and learning new things about buying and selling property that I hadn't been privy to in the past. The basics of real estate were another topic that should be taught in school or at least at the kitchen table at dinnertime with the family. I would pick his brain and jump at the chance to be nosy and learn whatever seemed most interesting in his day-to-day real estate adventures. I walked through some beautiful homes and some not-so-beautiful but practical for the client. I learned the flow of floor plans, as well as the proper names of certain rooms or upgrades in the house. Water Closet (the proper name when the toilet is in a separate room in the bathroom) and mudroom (the area usually by the garage just before entering the home where people decompress and remove shoes, hats, and jackets) were two of my newfound real estate terms. This was getting more and more interesting, and I began to gain a deeper interest in the business. I am a people person, so getting to know more people and helping them to secure one of the biggest purchases of their life would be rewarding. I think the thing that solidified my interest was witnessing a commission check. I had been paid 100% commission for most of my working life, so that part wasn't new. The new part, however, was once I got that check, I could move on to my next client, and that deal was done. No monitoring the business or making sure people paid made this sound like a great income stream addition.

I expressed my interest in adding real estate to my portfolio, and of course, Davis walked me through the process. I signed up for real estate school shortly after and focused solely on real estate for the next couple of months. I did this during the off-season for insurance so that I could give it most of my attention. It was 75 long, detailed, sometimes confusing hours of real estate and real estate law. I went to class 3 days a week and participated in study groups weekly. I listened to YouTube videos and asked Davis 1000 questions. I had successfully obtained many licenses and certifications in the past, but this one was definitely a challenge. At the end of the 75 hours, I took the prelicensing class test, and I passed! It was now time to sign up and take the state exam. I heard horror stories about people taking it repeatedly before they passed or just gave up. There were 2 parts to pass, so I studied for about a week and then went to see where my brain stood on real estate. I answered the last question and clicked submit only to find out that............................. I passed; Both sections; The first time! Let's make this money. I paid the 4-digit fees to start up, ordered business cards, got my email address and my real estate phone number, and I was ready to go.

My first client was a friend, and it was exciting and scary to go through my first process as an agent. Davis walked me through each task, and I soaked up all of the instructions. I learned how to fill out contracts and how to communicate with each party involved. I realized much of the class instruction through the hands-on training I now experienced. I learned about due diligence dates and closing dates now with practical application, and I learned how to get through complaints and put out fires when certain parties were unhappy. It was all so exciting! One of the most exciting parts was the commission check; finally, I was at the finish line. Deal #1 done; now on to the next one.

I've been a coach and a teacher for as long as I can remember. Coaching people through life is definitely at the top of "what is Autrina's purpose in this lifetime" list. I coached my friends on the playground when they were trying to figure out the maze. I coached my classmates in elementary when we had to complete group projects and when they were fighting with a friend and couldn't figure out conflict resolution. I was the spokesperson when it was time to talk about an assignment in class, and I volunteered for any program that allowed me to be a leader. I coached my cousins on how to get our parents to let us go outside or get something off the ice cream truck. I coached the softball team when our hired coach was busy doing something else, and I encouraged the team if we lost a game. I coached my younger siblings through their entire childhood, and I even coached some of the adults in my life when adulting made them frustrated. I coached our graduating class when we couldn't quite get the order of the program right, and I volunteered at freshman orientation in college. I've coached spouses, friends, family, business partners, church members, program coordinators, and, most importantly, clients.

Chapter 15
Put Me In The Game Coach

It's always been easy for me to go to a client's home to educate them about life or health insurance and spend an extra hour teaching them about taxes or college applications for their children. I've never successfully been able to only talk to a client or a friend only about the topic that started the conversation. I have gained so much knowledge in my 18 years of business, coupled with my genuine desire to elevate, which makes every moment a teaching moment. Insurance plans and investment accounts can be affected by many other aspects of your life, and just selling someone a product has never given me any satisfaction. If you fail to plan, you plan to fail, so if I don't educate you about the entire plan, I feel it's an injustice. There have been many occasions where I end up helping to fill out a scholarship application or giving insight on how to fill out the FAFSA. Because of the new health insurance improvements and the tax credits, I have found myself helping my clients set up businesses by giving them each step and where to go to complete them. The United States favors small business, and that is where you get the most benefits as far as taxes, grants, loans, and credit is concerned. I personally figured this out a while back, and of course, I have to share it with everyone that I encounter that could be doing it better.

I have spent countless hours helping with discovery and carrying out visions and plans for free. It got so bad that I knew I should be getting some type of compensation, so I just started charging a small consultation fee, but I still ended up doing a bulk of the work for free. Something had to give, and this was the start of the birth of my 3rd business. I decided to do small business coaching, so I created a business plan and a contract to make it legitimate. It still seemed like I was winging it, so I slowed down and returned to my teachings. For you to master anything new, you should have a mentor. Although I knew a magnitude of information about various business fields, I've never been an official business or life coach. I'm sure I could have continued to use trial and error and figured it out on my own, but that's not what I learned or was taught to get to where I am in business today.

I expressed my desire during a chat with my fiancé, and he encouraged me to push forward with my coaching business. I had found a way to combine all the knowledge I've acquired over the years with my nurturing, counseling, and teaching nature and create the ultimate mixture of life-changing literacy. The first step was to meditate and affirm my desires, followed by continuous prayers of gratitude until the Universe completed the perfect formula.

Not even a month after the initial conversation with my fiancé, one of my play nieces invited me to celebrate with her at an intimate birthday dinner. Only a handful of people were there, but the guest included her mom. Her mom, Tonia, just happened to be a renowned Success Mentor and Life Coach. Well, would you looka there, that's the Universe working its magic as usual. We were just having a general chat when I began to share my businesses and expertise in my fields. I expressed interest in starting a coaching business, and she informed me that I was in the right place at the right time. She used words and phrases like uplevel, manifest, powerhouse, eminence, feminine energy, total woman, divine purpose, and unleash your inner money maker, just to name a few. I was completely blown away, and I assured her that we would be having another conversation very soon. When we spoke again, I had what seemed like a million things going on, and she just encouraged me to trust myself and The Most High and stop second-guessing this next level. I had asked for it, and it had manifested.

I anxiously but confidently invested monetarily and timewise to make this goal come to fruition. I trusted her leadership and expertise to mentor and guide me through the unknown, and it has been one of the best decisions I have ever made. I started my 12-month program digging into my life from childhood to adulthood and my "why." I filled out packets, and she made the content clear, helping me understand how to connect the dots and how our thoughts become things. We did weekly coaching calls that helped me stay on track and make sure that this task wasn't lost in the sauce of my daily life. She gave me deadlines but taught me to give myself grace and be patient in the process. She reminded me that although my masculine process has been necessary to accomplish much of what I had in business, the balance of femininity is oh so sweet to bring it all together. She reminded me that my beauty and softness refined the lines of the painting, and being a total woman helped me see the other side of the road. Slowing down was something that I hadn't done much of because I was always focused on getting things done but coaching someone on their overall life takes patience and reading in between lines that they don't even see. I have a heart and a passion for women, and I realize that in order to reach and relate to the majority, I have to have the ability to mix the masculine and the feminine to create a perfect balance and a successful outcome.

Once she bulldozed my linear way of thinking when it came to business, I was able to move to the next step. Now I can figure out the scheduling and the business plan and the website and the photo shoot and how much to charge and how many packages to have and what's the verbiage on the email and what to say on social media and the many other things that we needed to do to make this vision run like a well-oiled machine. We were scheduling all of that and solidifying the launch date when I decided to finish this book and put it in the mix as well.

So now it is about the middle of September, and I have decided to take all of my brain dumps and all of my quotes, all of my experience, and all of my ideas, visions, and thoughts and complete the book that I have been aspiring to write and jot down points for and talking about for about five years now. I told her my plan, and she was like, "Really?" So now we had to set a date for the launch of the coaching business. I decided to call it Be Intentional with Autrina, and we had to schedule the photo shoot as well as securing the venue, as well as creating my packages, as well as hiring a website person to either do a landing page or a website.

We also had to find all my looks or outfits for my photo shoot, as well as secure the makeup artists, and I was going to do all of this while I was finishing a book. So, I planned to take a weekend and go out of town alone, in solitude, to finish as much of the book as possible. I decided to go to Clearwater, Florida.

The ocean is my safe haven, and I knew that that was the best place for the best mental energy for me to finish. So, I decided two weeks before the trip that I would go on October 7th and come back home on October 10th. I booked a flight and did not book a room until the day before my trip. My daughter was coming home from college to visit that same weekend and was leaving on Wednesday, so I also had to book her flight and make sure that everything was set up for her when she came home.

I am fortunate enough to have a phenomenal fiancé that made sure that everything was going to be okay while I was gone. I arrived in Clearwater on Friday at about 2:30, and by the time I was settled in my room, it was about five o'clock. I had to tie up some loose ends with my other businesses, and after that, I started writing. It was now about 6:30 PM, and I wrote until after midnight. The first day was finished, and I still had about 30,000 words to write. For the next two days, I planned to write for 12 hours, have four hours of downtime, and sleep for eight hours.

On Saturday, I woke up at 8:30 AM and started writing by 9:00. I didn't take my first break until about 2:30 when I went downstairs to the hotel and found some lunch. I was on break for about an hour and a half and started writing at about four o'clock. I wrote from four until eight o'clock, and I took another break to chat with Davis and clear my brain a little. I started writing back at 9:00 PM, and I wrote again until 12:30 AM. I went to sleep and slept eight hours and got up at 8:30 AM on Sunday morning to start back writing.

I was at approximately 12,000 words when I started on Sunday morning, and I wrote until about 5:00 PM before I took my first break. I broke to eat for the first time Sunday, and I finally walked to the beach for the first time since I arrived in Clearwater. It was very convenient because I was actually at the Hilton Resort & Spa, and I was oceanfront. I took a break from 6:00 PM to 7:00 PM to eat, walk to the beach, and then walk back to the room so that I could proceed with my writing.

I made a couple of phone calls to my daughter and to Davis, and I proceeded to continue writing at about 8:00 PM. I decided to write until 12:30, and that would be the night.

Chapter 16
Give Yourself Grace

They are all grown up now, and they are leaving for college. What am I going to do? My entire life has been centered around being a mommy. The entrepreneur part was highly important, but the mommy part was non-negotiable. My entire life, my why was my children and everything I did surrounding them. All my fun and excitement was transporting them back and forth to extracurricular activities, going to school events, and doing whatever they needed me to do at the moment to cause joy. I worked for them. I shopped for them. I went to restaurants for them. Everything was for them. Now they're older, have friends, want to go places without me, pick out their own clothes, and don't want my input in many of the decisions they make. My daughter is famous for saying, "Mommy, you taught us what to do; now you have to let us do it."

I have been an adult for a very long time, but now being an adult feels different because I can focus primarily on me. This feels something like a crisis, but I know it's just me trying to revamp my day-to-day intentions. I have a wonderful life and a wonderful fiancé. We travel, we eat frequently, and we go to concerts and shows. We hang out with our friends, have game nights at our house, and love each other constantly, whether that be laying around and watching an episode of Sanford and Son, or sitting on the back patio on the swing, watching the dogs run around and play. My life is phenomenal, so I'm not complaining; I am just recognizing the change.

I want to tell all the mommies in this chapter to give themselves grace. If you wanted to do things differently and you didn't have a chance to, it's okay. Start wherever you are now and recognize that as long as you're still breathing, you're still on the journey. The destination is far away because the journey will bring about destination after destination and more destinations to come. Whether your children are not born yet, toddlers, school age, adolescents, young adults, or adults, you still have time to influence them throughout the journey. The most important part of the journey is what you do to train your mind. Once you train your mind and you are able to lead by example, your example is more powerful than any words or instructions that you can give.

If your children are grown, the perfect place to start would be with your grandchildren—the ones you have and the ones that will come. You can start at the birth to infant phase and matriculate through their life and putting every lesson learned and perfecting every topic taught. The goal is to influence your heirs and generations to come. It doesn't matter where you start; it only matters how you finish. Remember, failing is not death, and until you quit, you can still win. Fail big and fail forward, and success is still within reach. You don't have to do everything at the same time either. If you have a business already, get a mentor. Find someone that specializes in your field, whether it is virtually, in a book, on a podcast, in person, or however you are able to reach that knowledge of improving your business. If you need hands-on training, find somebody that you trust to help you with your business.

If you desire to have a business, do the same thing, get a mentor and focus on your vision and your plan, and don't stop until you succeed. You may have a desire to lose weight. Get a mentor, find a system and a plan, and get started today. If you fall off, start over and have grace on yourself every time you start over. Until you quit, you haven't failed. You may want to save some money or buy a home or get a life insurance policy or get a health insurance policy. Get a mentor or find an expert and make sure you understand it and you do it correctly instead of just doing it.

If you want to fix your credit, find a credit specialist. Learn how credit works and find the time to do it slowly but surely. If you still have children and want to work on any of these goals, the best thing to do to cultivate your babies is to do it with them. Include them on your journey, include them as you search for a home, include them as you learn about credit, include them when you go to the bank, and you learn how to save money, include them when you're starting your business. Children are sponges, and they're very intelligent. They soak up anything you introduce to them and soak up whatever environment they're in the most. Make learning fun, and you could even make it into a game. Allow them to have input when you are accomplishing or working on a task.

None of us was born with a handbook, so as you read all my suggestions, the most important thing is to give yourself grace. If you have failed at most of what we are talking about, give yourself grace and start now on your journey to success. If you haven't started anything to fail, then now is the time to start. So, give yourself grace and move forward.

One of the areas that I have never been very knowledgeable about is how to build my credit. I knew some of the basic things about credit, and I knew that I struggled a little bit with credit because of life and the effects of divorce, as well as building my business and sacrificing one debt for another, but I didn't fully understand how credit worked. I put the energy in the universe so that I could fix it before it was too late to teach my children. I wanted to make sure that I was the example I didn't have going into young adulthood.

When I met Davis, one of the first things we talked about was how he got his credit score into the high 800s and almost a perfect score. I was eager and ready to learn. I immediately began to research and find credit specialists that could guide me through how to repair my credit. I started out with a credit score of less than 600, and the fight was on. The credit specialist helped me to get collections and derogatory marks removed, and I called companies to set up payment plans for items that could not be removed.

It took me about one year to clean up my credit to the point of applying for additional credit. I learned that the most important part of your credit report is for it to be clear of collections, late payments, and inquiries. After it was clear, the next thing to do was to build a credit history and trust with creditors. One of the best ways to gain history, if you don't have it yourself, is to become an authorized user on the credit card or credit line of someone who has a long positive credit history.

Since then, I have become much more well-versed at learning the credit formula. My credit score is in the high 700s, and the 800 benchmark is right around the corner. I went from having no available credit to well into six figures of available credit. I am not afraid anymore when I fill out credit applications, and it always comes back with approval. Credit is another topic that is not discussed in school or at the kitchen table in most low to middle income households.

Culturally, I only knew credit in the sense of utility bill deposits and rent-to-own stores. Credit cards were unheard of, and loans were only obtained through subprime lenders. I grew up thinking that money was the only part of wealth, and that's all I needed to focus on. However, I have been enlightened to know that credit is power, and if not more powerful, just as powerful than having money. Credit affords you simple conveniences, such as renting a car with one form of ID and no deposit. Credit saves you hundreds or even thousands of dollars when making purchases because interest rates are much lower with good credit. Credit removes the requirement for down payments and makes for a smoother process in every situation. Once I mastered personal credit, I began to study and research business credit, and that just opened up a floodgate of opportunity. Business credit is one of the major perks of doing business the right way.

So now, my goal was to be added to a card or credit line as an authorized user. Davis assisted me with this task and allowed me to be added to a couple of his credit cards. After removing everything derogatory and being added to establish credit, including trade lines, my credit began to improve greatly. Before, I would hold my breath before applying for credit, and I remember the first time I applied for a credit card after working on my credit, I got approved immediately. It was a credit card with Best Buy. Wasn't that ironic? Best Buy is where I met Davis, and after he helped me gain knowledge on fixing my credit, that was where I went to get my first credit card.

When I checked my credit, my score had gone from below 600 to the high 600s. Not long after, I was able to add another card to my credit profile, and roughly six months later, my credit score had broken 700. I was so happy, not just because I was gaining in the credit world, but because I was doing it in time to teach my children how to start their creditworthiness the right way.

I now have over six figures in business credit as well, and my biggest purchase solely with the use of my business was a 2022 Mercedes CLS. I bought this car for my business, and it is not attached to my personal credit. I bought it with no down payment and a very low interest rate. I bought it on my terms.

Let me give you a little more description of how this purchase went.In April of 2021, I walked into the Mercedes-Benz car lot and told them I wanted a Mercedes-Benz CLS with an AMG package. I don't know if they thought I was serious or not, but I wanted to build the car myself. So I went on the Mercedes-Benz website and built the car from start to finish; the color, the interior, the massage seats, the heated and cooled seats, everything that you can imagine that could be in the car is in the car. I designed the car and told them exactly what I wanted, and they told me that it would take about six to nine months for it to be built due to COVID-19. There was a microchip shortage.

The car was right at $100,000, and I confidently confirmed my build. I didn't know exactly how the purchase would go, but I knew that that was my desire and that I could manifest whatever I wanted as long as I did the work. So my co-collaboration with the universe was in action. It took about a year, and April 21st, 2022, is when I picked up my car. The salesman at the Mercedes car lot called me about two weeks before I received my car and told me that it was on the boat on the way to me. When I got that phone call to go and pick it up, I was super excited.

When I got to the car lot, everybody was waiting for me. It was the first 2022 CLS AMG to appear on the lot. It is snow-white with a fire red interior, and it is hot! They had dealers, service people, clients, and everybody that you could think of surrounding MY car. This little girl from Gastonia, North Carolina that grew up in the 'hood, was about to purchase a car with a tag over $100,000. My dream car, to say the least. We went through the entire process. I let them know that I was buying this car through my business and that I did not want my personal information to be attached, and they did everything I asked them to do the way I asked them to do it. I bought a full bumper-to-bumper warranty on the car, including service and tires. For the next four years, I don't have to spend one penny on maintenance, scratches, dents, or any of the like.

I drove off that car lot with such a sense of pride for myself and my journey. I can't turn back now, and it's only up from here.

While we're on the subject of credit, let's go back to the children. We should be teaching them about credit from the very beginning. Small things like just making sure you do what you say you're going to do is the first lesson of credit. When my children were young teens, I began to teach them the importance of paying their debts and not getting into debt in the first place. When I would pay my utility bills or my car payment, or my insurance, as well as any other debt, I would include them in the process and explain to them that we are paying Duke Power to keep lights on, and if we don't pay them, they will turn off our lights.

I would explain to them that if we didn't make our car payment, they would come and take the car back, and we had to do this until we had paid the entire amount from the initial purchase. I would also sit my children down and explain to them the budget for our household. When they were playing sports or involved in extracurricular activities, I would not hide from them the cost of the activities, especially when there was traveling involved, such as travel baseball or camps or summer programs out of town.

When they were little, they thought what most children think about the availability of money. They would ask for something and then remind me, "Mom, all you have to do is go to the ATM and get the money out." As they got older, I taught them that the money has to come from you working hard and you put the money in the bank so that they can give it to you when you go to the ATM; or you pay people when you say you're going to pay them, and then they trust you and allow you to buy things on credit.

While they can't have an individual bank account until age 18, most banks will allow you to set up a custodial or joint bank account for your children at about age 13 or older. Around that age, I took Micah and Michael to the bank, and we did just that. I let them sit through the whole process, create their own PIN numbers for their debit cards, and add online banking apps to their phones. I gave them money now only through their bank accounts and showed them how to save money in their savings accounts.

This was a way to make them aware of what was going in and coming out instead of having the ease of just transferring money from my hand to theirs. This was subconsciously teaching them to be responsible and to set up a bank account, a savings account, and soon an investment account for their earnings. It is also important to establish credit for your children at a young age, and I'm not talking about the credit of putting the light bill in their name or the cable bill in their name because your credit is not good enough to use your own Social Security number.

That is what I was used to seeing growing up in the neighborhoods I grew up in. I added both of my children as authorized users on the longest credit card with the best standing I had established. One of the biggest parts of the credit score calculation is the longevity of good standing accounts, so adding them to cards around the age of 15 created a three-year automatic credit history by the time they were 18. This also helps because they have a credit history without any inquiries, so it's only positive credit. By 18, they both had two credit cards in their name with a long and positive history, and this allowed them to be able to start young adulthood at the top and not at the bottom.

Chapter 17
Buying The Kids A Car

I bought the kids their first car. Michael got a 2000 Lexus RX350 SUV, and Micah got a 2007 Lexus ES300 car. Michael's car served him well for about three and a half years before it began to give him trouble. He drove it until the wheels fell off, about 100+ miles a day, to say the least. He had it to begin college, and he would drive it back and forth from Burlington, North Carolina, to Lake Norman frequently. It started to become too much of a maintenance issue, and he decided he wanted to just buy a new car. So here comes the lesson on good credit. I sat him down and taught him how to buy a car; I explained to him that because his credit score was above 780, he would be able to buy whatever he wanted that was in his price range. I explained to him that he would not have to pay a down payment and could buy it on his terms.

My son is his mama's child; therefore, he has always had a job as long as I allowed it, and he has always worked hard, whether for employment or personal accomplishments. We researched several different car makes and models to see what would be the most efficient vehicle for his needs. We test drove several, and the Honda, Toyota, Lexus, and Kia were among his top choices. We test drove the Camry LE, and he enjoyed the ride but didn't really like the bulky style of the Camry; he said it seemed too much like a family car. The last car that we tested out was the brand-new Kia K5 GT-line. Again, because my children have been taught to be grateful for and expect what they desire in life, he decided that he wanted a black Kia K5 with a red leather interior, and he wouldn't accept anything else.

So, of course, we found the car he wanted, it was the last one on the lot, and he test drove and fell in love with it. The salesperson helping us with this car invited us into the lot to have a seat and figure out the details of the purchase. We let him know from the beginning what we were planning to pay, put down, and the monthly payment amount desired. The sales guy was an older white gentleman, and he spoke directly to my 19-year-old son at the time, asking him exactly how he was planning to make this purchase. My son told him that the purchase would be made solo and that he would not be putting any money down. The sales guy started talking to me and suggested that I co-sign for Michael and maybe consider putting some money down. I was puzzled as to why he disregarded the instructions given to him by my child and thought it necessary to instruct me on how I needed to help him.

I guess this is what was common during a car deal with a 19-year-old, but unbeknownst to him, we are not common people at all. I reiterated to the sales guy that what my son told him initially was what we were doing. He would be purchasing the car independently with no co-signer and would not need to put a payment down. I insisted that instead of continuing to have a back-and-forth conversation, we move forward to finance and let them check his credit and then let us know the terms of the agreement. It took about 20 minutes for the sales guy to stop asking us questions about our intentions and take our application to his finance department.

I almost had to complain and get more stern than I had hoped for in order to get beyond the questioning and move ahead to finishing the deal. Once the sales guy retreated and got our application to finance, it took about 10 minutes for us to be greeted by the finance manager to let us know what our options were. He and three other guys first came to greet my son and congratulate him on his creditworthiness as well as his poise and professionalism in his attempt to purchase a new vehicle on his own. No one could believe that he was only 19, and he was able to walk into the car lot and create his own terms, and, oh yeah, that he was a melanated male.

To make a long story a little shorter, Michael was able to purchase this 2022 Kia K5 GT-line vehicle with no down payment and no co-signer. He requested that they move faster because we had been at the lot much longer than we needed to be, and we went into the finance manager's office so that he could autograph all the documents.

When the whole process was over, it had to be one of the happiest that I had ever seen him; he was full of pride and so grateful for the opportunity to reward himself with his manifestations. He got in his black sports car with his red leather interior and drove off the lot like a boss. I was one proud mom.

Bonus topic:

Sometimes my children remind me of what I've taught them. I recall taking my daughter back to the airport after a weekend break from college. We were supposed to wake up at 6:30 AM to catch a 9:30 flight, but it didn't quite go that way. I woke up and looked at the clock, and it was 7:16 AM, "Aw man, I'm late." So I jumped up and went to wake Micah up; she said that she was already packed and just had to get dressed. I told her that we had to leave as soon as possible, and I jumped in the shower to get dressed as well. We finally ran out of the door, threw the bags in her trunk, and sped out of the neighborhood.

It was now 7:35, and my GPS said it was going to take us 42 minutes to get to the airport. I began to panic and told Micah that we may not make it in time for her to check her bags and catch her flight. Micah immediately looked at me and chastised my thought process. "Mommy!" she exclaimed, "Are you serious right now? You already know that we're going to make it in time; the universe is going to work it out where all the traffic is flowing, and when we get to the airport, everybody will be courteous and helpful, and we will get checked in on time. Why would you put negativity into the universe? That energy is not going to manifest us getting to the airport on time."

I was immediately humbled and almost joyful at the lesson that my daughter reminded me of. As I smiled, I drove mostly the speed limit, and the highways opened up for us. We made it to the airport in time and just so happened to be able to check her bag in outside at the valet check-in. She had over an hour to spare as she went into the airport and was able to comfortably get through security and to her gate. "Mommy, I'm glad I was with you on the way to the airport because you would not have made it without me and my positive energy," Micah called me as she was boarding her flight, and I continued to be grateful for the subconscious mind that my children have been blessed to obtain.

Preface To The Co-Writers Chapters:

So, I had this idea because, as parents, sometimes we think we know what our children are thinking, what they would do in a situation, what they would not do in a situation, or just how they are as a whole. I thought I would test out my theory of training your children and leading by example by allowing them to participate in this book.

I asked my children to share a chapter of their life with the world, with other Mommypreneurs, other children, and their peers. I asked them to write a chapter, and I gave them no direction. I told them to write about anything that came to their mind regarding their childhood. It could be at any point of their childhood, whether it is the toddler phase, grammar school phase, high school phase, or even young adulthood now that they have matriculated to college.

Both of them asked me for more insight and what I would have them write about, but I would not give them anything to go on because I truly wanted to just see what came from their hearts and if my ideas on what raising them the way I did were accurate or not.

My son is very detailed, organized, and very much a perfectionist. He almost has perfection anxiety at times, and he is my straight-line child that is going to do everything by the books. He is alpha in every sense of the word and as masculine as you can imagine. Because of this personality, he questioned me over and over and over, "Mommy, what do you want us to write about? I need some direction." He said that he needed to know a little bit about the book so that he could make sure that he was in one accord with what I was writing. He also said that he didn't want his chapter to be off or sound like it didn't fit in with the book. He just asked me every which way you could think of to get me to give him some direction on what to write about, and still, I did not budge. I truly wanted to get his perspective on whatever story, timeframe, or season of his life he chose to write about. I did not want his chapter to be biased in any way. He finally stopped asking me a bunch of questions and just decided to write the chapter on whatever he could come up with.

My daughter, on the other hand, is my artist, as I have described to you in the above chapters. She did not ask a second time or care to know what my portion of the book was going to be about, and that is typical Micah. She has always been my flowy child, my free-in-the-wind, artsy, get it however I get it child. She has always been my child that would rather ask for forgiveness instead of permission because what she wants to experience in life, she insists on experiencing it by any means necessary. I absolutely support her personality because it is who she is, and although my parenting may have touched each of my children differently, I must say, and I must believe that it did touch them.

If I had to guess, the chapter that Michael writes versus the chapter that Micah writes would have a very different flow, but that's what makes them who they are, and that's what makes me so excited to be their mommy.

Chapter 18
(Michael's Chapter)
Mama's Boy

I think for the start of my chapter, I will introduce myself. I haven't had any sneak peeks into the book, so I have no idea what you guys know me as, but everyone calls me Michael. I don't remember exactly what it means, but I know it is derived from the bible and was primarily chosen because in my childhood, I was raised in the church, and my mom has been in a church all her life. Secondly, my nickname is VJ. So although I introduce myself as Michael, all my closest family and friends address me by my nickname. It's been this way since I was little. At home, I am VJ, but at school or anywhere else, for the most part, I am known as Michael, and every once in a while, when my sister is mad or annoyed at me, she will call me Michael. No one besides my family understands where the VJ comes from, but when I break it down, it makes perfect sense. Basically, my middle name is Veshaun which is where the V comes from, and I am a junior which is where the J comes from. I don't know how old I will be when this book finally comes out, but right now, I am twenty years old. And for the twenty years I have been living, I can say that my mom has been the number one person in my life.

In every aspect of the word, I am a mama's boy. I act just like my mom. We think alike. I even think that, in some ways, she thinks I probably take it to the extreme. This can be a good or a bad thing at times. For one, we both are overthinkers. We think of one hundred scenarios in situations that people probably haven't even thought of. It's kind of weird, though, because, at the same time, we are very laid back and easygoing about most things. We don't make big deals out of problems because, in the grand scheme of things, whatever is happening doesn't matter. Next, we both are very intelligent, and we have street smarts as well, but we do have our slow moments every once and a while. Like we sometimes make statements in the form of questions which to the people around us can get annoying. Besides thinking alike, we have the same hairstyle and look alike. When I say we are identical, I mean like people who don't even know we are related often put two and two together. Finally, we went everywhere together. I was always up under my mom. Whether in baseball games, going to the store, at her business appointments, or anything else, I was with my mom. Some kids would tell their parents to stop being lovey-dovey when their friends are watching, but I have always been the complete opposite. If you couldn't tell by looking at us, there would be no question of whose kid I was because I made sure everybody knew, and I was proud of it. And at 20 years old, I am still the same way, just a little bit taller and a little bit better looking. Honestly, thinking back on my childhood, I have nothing to complain about. I think my mom tried her best and put me in the best positions I needed to be in to succeed, but besides the doors she was able to open for me, like putting me in a great school and keeping wherever I was stable, I think the most important thing I was gifted from her was my mindset. I believe that even if I was not privileged enough to experience the things I did as a child and be presented with the opportunities I had, with the mindset I have inherited from my mother, I still would be able to make the best out of any situation. The two most important things I have learned in my childhood are gratitude and accountability.

One thing she never tolerated was anyone being ungrateful, especially me and my sister, Micah, because everything we needed, and if we wanted something, we were usually able to get it. In my childhood, I was never materialistic anyway, so all I wanted to do was play sports. So, there wasn't a reason not to be grateful in the first place, and if we were ungrateful, we were reminded that everything we got to do could be taken away immediately. She would say, "You don't have to do anything I pay for you to do if you don't appreciate it…. You can just go to school and go home every day." Personally, I never wanted to test my mom, so I fell in line quickly, but my sister was more of a rebel, so I think her lessons were usually a little harder than mine growing up. To put it in layman's terms, she got in trouble more than I did, but back to the point; I think this reminder that the extra things that we did were privileges was all we needed to understand that whatever our circumstances are every day we wake up is a privilege. So although we have completely different personalities, my sister and I both recognize the privilege we have and are very grateful every day to be able to experience life.

Also, my whole family, including my mom, is from the south. I don't understand how other people are raised, but all I know is to say please and thank you. Southern hospitality is a real thing. Any little thing someone does for me, even if they are supposed to do it, I say thank you and show gratitude. I think this is one of the biggest things that help me remember to just be grateful. I have been this way since I was a kid, though. I don't know any other way to be and am honestly reminded every day that everyone is not raised the same way. If I had a dollar for the number of times my mom was complimented on my manners when I was younger, I would be rich right now. As a matter of fact, people have literally offered to give me money for how nice I have been as a kid and for doing things like opening doors for them. These little lessons of gratitude that I have learned as a kid, I take with me everywhere I go and in everything I do. I think with more gratitude comes more happiness. It is very hard to be grateful and unhappy at the same time. Not that it is impossible, but for the most part, if you are thinking about how grateful you are for something or someone, it is going to be hard to at the same time be sad or mad. Regardless of what is going on, I try to be grateful for every little thing I can. I look at my family and my friends, and I'm grateful; it's a nice day outside, and I'm grateful. I ate some good food, and I am especially grateful! I have learned to be grateful every day for the little things that go right and that I can control instead of focusing on the things that go wrong or that I cannot control because, honestly, that doesn't help anything. Most people who know me would usually say that I am nonchalant, easygoing, goofy, and happy, and this mindset is why.

The other thing that my mother has taught me is accountability. I am sure most parents have told their kids that it is nothing they can't do as well as the cliche saying to "follow your dreams." Well, my mom has also done this, but I think she has done it through her actions and in a more realistic manner. For one, I have gotten a front row seat to see my mom follow and fulfill her dreams and anything she sets her mind to. This book is one of them. I remember going to the Primerica meetings where they constantly said, "Super great, getting better everyday," with a little oomf at the end. I remember going to her insurance appointments where the clients knew who I was. I remember listening to business calls my mom was on and meeting a lot of her business partners. I think this up-close point of view of my mom's entrepreneurial journey has helped me not only believe the saying follow your dreams, but also helped me see someone doing it for 20 years of my life. I think someone telling you to do something is great, but when you can see them doing it themselves is all the better. Watching her reach her goals makes me want to set my own goals and gives me ambition.

I think watching my mom work so hard also taught me something that is needed in a person, which is accountability. How can I improve, what can I do better, did I do what I said I was going to do, and am I working to be the person I said that I am and that I want to be? My mom has always preached to me that honestly, she doesn't care if I want to be the richest person in the world or a regular person who has a decent job, but whatever I do, I have to be accountable for my own future. Regardless of what I have decided to do rather than play baseball or go to college or start a business, my mom has always supported me but then asked me what's the plan and how am I going to hold myself accountable. I don't blame anyone or anything for my problems. I never have, and I never will. That doesn't help me or make anything better. Instead, I was taught to ask myself what needs to be done to fix whatever isn't working and to remedy any issue. What is in my power so that I can do the things that I want to do with my life, and the answer is everything is in my power. I get to decide how hard I work and what I put my effort into. Thanks to this mindset, I have all the control over my life.

I remember the first time I told my mom that I wanted to be an entrepreneur. I was 14 and in the 8th grade. I just couldn't see myself working for someone all my life because I, for one, don't want anyone telling me what I have to do, and for two, that wasn't what I was used to, seeing my mom always work for herself. My journey with entrepreneurship started one night when I thought my mom was taking me home from baseball practice. I told her I wanted to start a boy's formal wear clothing business. I am still very much into fashion, but at this time, I specifically liked formal wear and wanted to focus on helping boys dress as freshly as men do when it came to formal wear. Of course, she supported me, but from then on, I had to create a plan of the things I wanted and needed to do to make this work. So basically, at 14 years old, I learned about an elevator pitch, I had to come up with a specific design, and I created a slogan which was

"Dress to Impress." I was only 14 and didn't know a lot, but with my mom's guidance and my creativity, I was able to learn a lot about entrepreneurship. I think the most important thing that I learned is the amount of work it takes to be an entrepreneur. But from that moment, with my mom's help, I was able to do a few local fashion shows, sell some products, and design my own clothing line. I think with the privilege of having my mom and being able to do things like this, it just increased my interest in business and working for myself. From this point in my late childhood, I have been interested in the life of an entrepreneur and hardworking people in general. Other than my mom's influence, I have also been able to take influences from other business people and hardworking people in general, but quite frankly, I think Entrepreneurship and accountability go hand and hand. I think to be successful in entrepreneurship and in life, this concept of accountability is super important. I believe, along with gratitude, accountability is one of the reasons I think my mom's influence is so important in my childhood and the rest of my life. I believe that if you take accountability for every aspect of your life, especially parts that would be easy for you to blame others, you can control much more of your happiness. If you are the reason for things going good or bad, then that means you are the only thing you need to keep things good or make things in your life better, which is a position I would rather be in and is the way my mom has been living her life since I can remember which is the only reason she is able to live life so freely and give me a worry-free childhood.

I think these two skills that my mom taught me just through her actions and lessons are the reason I am who I am today. Without trying to, I think my mom, in a way, raised the boy version of herself. I mean, there are obviously other influences, but because of my mom's lessons and her involvement in my life, her influence was the one that meant the most and made the most impact on me. Now I look to be able to use what she taught me and rub it off on other people and also bring people who think alike to me. Also, I hope to be able to use these skills to reach whatever goals I have.

Chapter 19
(Micah's Chapter)
My Hair

I have had a complicated relationship with my hair from a very young age. When I was little, I had very healthy hair. It was long, all the way down my back. When I was around six years old, I got a relaxer. At first, I loved it. I've always loved having long, flowing, straight hair that made me feel like all the princesses I grew up watching. Then my hair became damaged. We had to cut it up to my chin. I knew it was necessary so that my hair could grow back healthy again, but all I could really think about was my hair being taken from me. However, my mom never let me forget how beautiful I was. She made sure I had a new style every week. Braiding it, straightening it, putting beads in it, and doing whatever she could to make me feel beautiful even if my hair wasn't long anymore. Growing up with so many options and alleyways for creativity and expression is one reason I was able to feel beautiful after cutting my hair. Instead of a loss, my mom helped me see my new length as an opportunity to express my creativity and to better my ampleness for change. This skill, however, was truly put to the test during my ten years attending Woodlawn School.

When I was in the third grade, I began attending Woodlawn School, a small K-12 school with no more than 120 students at the time. When I joined, I was not only the singular black girl in my class but in the entire school. It stayed like this for the majority of my years attending, sometimes even being the only minority in the class. When I first enrolled at the age of eight, I was so excited to show all my white classmates the beauty of black hair. I would wear my hair in afros, Bantu knots, mohawks, and any cool style I could get my momma to do for me, no matter how much it hurt my head. I was even known for never having the same style for more than a week. I loved being the only person with my kind of hair. I remember girls asking if my mom could do their hair like mine and internally giggling because I knew their hair could never accomplish what my hair could. It made me feel beautiful, unique, and special. I continued to wear my hair like this through the entirety of my lower school years until puberty began to hit.

Just like any young girl going through the hell of puberty, I was scared and confused about the changes happening to me, and I became insecure. I began comparing myself to the girls around me, not only on TV and in the media, but also my peers and classmates that I was surrounded by every day. This way of thinking was especially harmful, considering I was surrounded by white women. I was so different from them in every way, and instead of seeing this as a gift, I saw it as a flaw. All I wanted was to be as beautiful as them. I decided that I couldn't change my skin color or how big my thighs were, but I could change my hair. The fifth grade was the last time I wore my hair in a natural style until my junior year of high school.

In middle school, I began to only wear my hair straight. I couldn't handle any other style. When my mom stopped having time to always straighten my hair, I began doing it myself. This was a terrible idea. I was so desperate to always have my hair straight that I would do anything to get it there, even if it meant damaging my curls. I would straighten and re-straighten my hair almost every day, the slightest bit of frizz or curl making me incredibly nervous to go to school or see my friends. On days when I couldn't tame the frizzy, damaged mess, I would put a hat on, still assuring that my straightened hair was able to be seen so that no one would think I was different. On top of this, the idea of getting my hair wet was a nightmare. Rainy school days or field days with water sports were instances of high intensity for me. I would wear hoods and always make sure I had an umbrella before going to school. I made sure to tell teachers ahead of time that I couldn't participate in activities that my peers were able to do out of fear of getting my hair wet. Luckily, I went to a pretty liberal school, so my teachers were very understanding about the fear I had of being stigmatized for my natural hair. Even so, my classmates and friends were confused, and some even mocked me, pretending to get my hair wet and judging me for not participating. Some even told me I was dramatic and overreacting; thinking back on times like that makes me a bit sad. I'm sad that I let other people's opinions stop me from having fun and being a kid like my peers. I'm sad that I spent days crying in the bathroom during class because I thought my hair made me look ugly. I'm especially sad that the anxiety about my image stunted my creativity for all those years.

As I grew older, many things changed for me. One thing that stayed constant, however, was the incoming comments from everyone around me about how beautiful my mother was. My entire life, my mother has dressed well, had beautiful hair, and had a smile that made other people smile. She truly was, and still is, one of the most beautiful women I have ever seen, and just about everyone around me agrees. As I grew older, I started receiving compliments about my appearance, many of these from people telling me that I looked like my mother. People would tell me that we had similar smooth complexions, similar body shapes, and similar smiles. I never really saw it myself. I told myself that people were lying to make me feel better. When I was younger, everyone told me I looked like my dad, and I agreed. Though I was confused and in denial of these compliments, I took it as an opportunity to begin allowing myself to feel beautiful again. Slowly going into high school, I began to appreciate myself more and find things that I love about myself. Instead of comparing myself to people I could never look like and had nothing in common with, I stopped comparing and used my mom as an inspiration to love myself. I began to love my body and get incredibly into fashion and experimenting with different ways to style my specific type of silhouette. Instead of hiding my face behind makeup, I learned to use makeup to accentuate the parts of my face that I loved so much. Once I saw the same beauty in my mother that I saw in myself, I slowly felt my creativity come back and learned to truly express myself again.

The last step of acceptance for me was accepting my hair. This was the longest and most difficult journey for me. Though I felt more comfortable, hair is still a very important and complicated part of every woman. For so long, women have used and been programmed to think of their hair as almost an extension of themselves. Many women see their hair as a form of expression and femininity and feel almost lost or less than without it. For me, not having long, straight princess hair made it hard for me to be comfortable with myself, my femininity, and my way of expression. This slowly began to change when a black girl entered my class in my sophomore year of high school. Her name was Nathalie. She had shared my similar experience of being the only black girl in her school, so we instantly clicked. At the end of our sophomore year, Nathalie and I teamed up to do a school project on being black girls in all-white schools. We shared our experiences with racism, insecurities, and our hair. We even did a whole video on wash days and styling. Though I wanted to be in the video with Nathalie, my insecurities would not allow me, and I decided to stay behind the camera. At the end of our Sophomore year, Nathalie was moving and leaving Woodlawn school. Before she left, Nathalie made me promise to begin wearing my hair naturally when Junior year began. I was incredibly hesitant, but something about spending those few months with Nathalie gave me the courage to say yes, and of course, my mom was all for it.

That summer, my mom helped me experiment with my hair. We tried new styles and products to find what worked best for my natural styles. Because, of the changes in my curls, from puberty and damage, it was a long journey. There were so many failed attempts and so many tears. I would feel so defeated sometimes, looking in the mirror and hating what I saw. A lot of times, I wanted to quit and just put in a weave to not have to deal with it, but I kept trying, and my mom was right there with me, telling me how beautiful I was with each new style I tried.

One day towards the end of that summer, my mom had to run some errands, and I was tagging along. Before we left the house, I asked her to help me take out some twists we had put in the night before. When we were finished, I was shocked. This was the first time in a very long time that I looked in the mirror and really loved my natural hair. I remember not being able to put my phone down or stop taking pictures of myself. I was so excited and so in love with my hair. I became so confident that I posted my hair on my Snapchat. I was so nervous to see what my classmates and friends would say about my new style. In no time, I began receiving comments from all of my friends about how much they loved my hair. I had never felt so confident in my own skin. That was an amazing feeling that I decided right then that I wanted to keep having.

In my junior year of high school, I walked in every week with a new hairstyle. Once again, I became known for this. That year and my Senior year were truly years of experimentation. I began doing all sorts of hairstyles I never had the courage to wear before out of fear of looking too different. I tried weaves, box braids, flat twists, cornrows, faux locs, and just about anything I could figure out how to do or get done. It felt amazing to once again use my hair as a form of expression and creativity. I hadn't felt so free since I was that little girl in third grade, coming into a new school with the biggest afro any of those kids had ever seen. Being able to become more comfortable and confident in my outside appearance definitely affected the way I began expressing myself. I saw myself go from a shy little girl, desperate to fit in and be liked, to a confident young woman who made her own place. I began speaking out and standing up for myself in aspects of my life where I had felt hopeless. As I grew more appreciative, I began to see even more of all those aspects of my mom that made people say that I looked like her. I saw our similarity in complexion, body shape, and, most of all, in our smiles. I realized I had the same warm smile and eyes as my mother. The type to make others smile. The kind of smile that makes people love and trust you. The kind of smile that makes people feel like everything is alright. I truly believe that we have these smiles because of our genuine hearts. My entire life, I've seen my mother be a lifeline. She will help family, friends, strangers, and anyone she believes has a good heart. Everywhere we went, I would see my mother making friends, making people smile, and radiating pure light and joy upon anyone who met her. No matter how much time or money we had, my mother would spare no expense to help someone in need. This is something that it took me a while to realize that my mother had embedded in my brother and me.

In my short life so far, I have learned a remarkable number of lessons. I have experienced deep emotions I never thought I could come out of. During this brief journey, I think the biggest lesson I've learned is the meaning of true beauty. It is no denying that my mother is absolutely stunning on the outside, but her beauty on the inside is incomparable. It is the true form of love and the reason why everyone is drawn to her so much. When people tell me I'm beautiful or that I look like my mother now, I believe them, and I thank them genuinely. Because they see the same light that radiates within my mother, within me. The funniest thing is I would have never accepted my light if I had never accepted my hair.

My Take:

Oh my God, that went exactly how I expected! I have only been a fly on the wall a few times in life and heard my children describe something as I would have had them describe it without me present. This was another time.

I really hope you enjoyed their chapters as much as I did. I was fascinated the entire time I was reading. It's different when you know who and how your children are versus when you actually listen to them speak or watch them react to a situation exactly the way you would have them do it. Michael's chapter was linear and strategic, just as I had imagined. He was still concerned about being accurate with everything and talking about business, accountability, and everything that would make sense in life when it came to him being successful. He wasn't so concerned about ... As usual, even in his chapter, he wants to make sure that he does everything right and perfectly. He wants to make sure that he is aligned with the vision, and he wants to make sure that he is making, first of all, himself proud. Although his chapter was nothing less than amazing, it was absolutely expected because of his linear and to-the-point personality.

Micah, on the other hand, always surprises me. Her surprises are always joyful, and they always make me gasp or comment that this girl is something else. I had no idea what to expect from Micah, but I knew that it would be a free and flowy topic and a topic that was unexpected. Micah's chapter about her hair is just what I expected. Without knowing exactly what she would write about, I knew that it would be something dealing with her artistic mindset. It could have been her eyes; it could have been about a friend that is bisexual. It could have been anything you can imagine, but it definitely was not going to be linear. I am so excited to be their Mom.

If you read the chapter about Micah and her hair and you internalize everything that she wrote, you will absolutely know who Micah is. She treats every subject and every part of life the same way. She explained how she went through her phases and her process of realizing her beauty. And once she realizes it, the rest is history.

These chapters show me and allow me to show everyone else that my children are nowhere close to perfect, and they have still gone through the stages of life with all the obstacles, all of the questions, and all of the challenges as any other child in the world. The difference, however, is their subconscious mind is always going to take them back to growth, manifestation, gratitude, accountability, and just being responsible for the outcome of their lives. I did not know what to expect from allowing them to write their chapters with no guidance, but I am extremely satisfied and honored by what they chose to share. My hope is that not only will parents and entrepreneurs read this book but also children, adolescents, and young adults, and I hope that this book changes someone's life or at least enlightens their journey.

Conclusion

It was September 2017, and We were standing on the sand bar in Stingray City. The water was like a crystal clear, massive bathtub, around 86 degrees, and it was one of the most beautiful sights I'd ever seen.

(Wikepedia, Stingray City) Stingray City is a series of shallow sandbars found in the North Sound of Grand Cayman Islands. It is a tourist attraction where stingrays are found in abundance, and visitors can pet and interact with the animals.

Although you are free to rent or take your own boat to Stingray City, we have a very skilled and knowledgeable guide. We were in the natural habitat of the Stingray animals, and the guide was able to safely handle them. I held the body of the Stingray, it laid on my back, and the best part was I kissed the Stingray! It is a legend that if you kiss a stingray on its head, you'll get seven years of good luck. The residents of Stingray City are comfortable around humans and are not alarmed by a quick kiss in exchange for some squid.

"Would you participate in a discovery scuba diving adventure?" Davis asked. "Umm, I can barely swim," I answered, "but will that stop me from being able to do it?" He assured me that being a great swimmer is not necessary when you are 30-40 feet under water with an oxygen tank on your back and a master diver with you at all times. All you have to do is learn a few skills to keep you safe under water and enjoy the magnificent barrier reefs of the clear turquoise waters of the Caribbean Ocean. I agreed, and he set it up. I went to the two-hour scuba training session, met my master scuba diving guide, and got fitted for snorkel, fins, scuba gear, and oxygen tank. Davis is already an advanced scuba diver and didn't need a chaperone. We started off in the natural pool (a shallow part of the ocean), and once I was comfortable with buoyancy and things of the like, we progressed into the great big ocean!

As we descended 10 ft, 15 ft, 20 ft, 25 ft, 30 ft. 35 ft, I saw sea life that was unimaginable. There were so many colorful fish, from tiny to massive. There was tuna, flounder, tarpons, grouper, angel fish, and shrimp just to name a few. I also had the pleasure of seeing more stingrays, lobster, crab, sea turtles, and guess what? I saw a shark! It was a nurse shark, and they are seemingly harmless. Of course, there were also countless sea life that I can't begin to describe. This experience was second to none and one that I'll never forget.

One morning we woke up and decided to go on an adventure without guides. We got a tip from the locals on where to experience swimming with the turtles in their natural habitat. It's called Spotts beach, and the turtles feed on seagrass every morning just after dawn. Wow is the best description I have! We were up close and personal with huge sea turtles. They were like the ones on Finding Nemo!

We also visited a place called Starfish Point. This is a nice public beach that is famous for having starfish lying around on the sandy beach. The water is very shallow and then drops off to about 10 feet deep. We snorkeled and were able to see many more of the starfish that settled in the deeper water. It looked like something that you would see on T.V.

One more…. We arrived at a horse ranch, and I was informed that we were going to go horseback riding on the beach. It was like something in a Romance Novel, and there was no one participating but me, my fiancé, and the guide. We were given a few instructions and assured that we would have an amazing adventure; just follow the guide. So, we set out on the street at first and, about a mile later, ended up on the beautiful white sand beach looking over the turquoise waters of the Caribbeans. We followed the guide for a bit, and then we stopped and were informed that he was going to unsaddle the horses. We were about to take the horses into the ocean; I had no idea that horses could swim. On the back of horses, walking in the middle of the ocean, staring as far as the eye can see at the line that appears to be a drop off in the abyss; this was paradise!

I had only experienced elaborate vacations or outings related to business travel. I had actually been out of the country before, but it was a company convention, and at the time, I could barely buy a hamburger, let alone participate in an excursion. Sadly, I barely even remember what the beach looked like or what being close to the ocean felt like on previous company trips.

This vacation was life-changing and reminded me of my worth and everything I'd worked for. It reminded me that I deserved everything that The Most High promised, and the Universe was like a genie just waiting for my command. Water has always been calming for me. I love hot summer days, and ocean sounds are magical. Being in this environment constantly and soon permanently definitely fits my destiny.

Whatever makes you tic is what you should set out to experience. You deserve it! The Universe says you can have it if you believe. All you have to do is affirm, attract and manifest. You are a mommy, an entrepreneur, a wife, a sister, an auntie, a friend, a mentor, a creator, and a partner. Hell, you give life! Go be the Goddess that you were created to be. Work smart, play hard, and decide how you would like your story to be written!

About The Author

Autrina Tillman is an 18+ year entrepreneur, blessed with two beautiful children: Michael and Micah. She started her educational adventures at Winston-Salem State University in May of 1996. She completed a Bachelor of Science degree in Biology and Chemistry in 2000 and started a career as an educator. 8th grade Math and Science was her home until she was introduced to the financial services world. Autrina has several licenses and certifications, including a life/health/Medicare insurance license. She is a licensed real estate broker and a certified life and business coach. She is also a certified travel agent and has successfully assisted her son in developing a clothing line. Autrina has trained and developed hundreds of people, managed millions in the investment world, and helped thousands of families with financial literacy. She has spoken at financial services conferences with thousands of attendees and imparted knowledge and mindset training that changed lives. Autrina is passionate about her craft, and her unsatisfactory conduct grade for talking in elementary school has been her biggest contribution to the Universe.

To Work With Autrina Tilman Scan The QR Code Below.

REFERENCES

Home. (2022, March 22). Real Diapers. Retrieved October 23, 2022, from https://realdiapers.org/

Home. (n.d.). City of Gastonia. Retrieved October 23, 2022, from https://www.cityofgastonia.com/

Gastonia, NC From Wikipedia, the free encyclopedia

https://en.wikipedia.org/wiki/Gastonia,_North_Carolina

King James Bible. (n.d.). Retrieved October 23, 2022, from http://kingjamesbible.com

Benefits of Breastfeeding - Capital Women's Care | MD, DC, & VA. (n.d.). Retrieved October 23, 2022, from https://www.cwcare.net/news/benefits-breastfeeding-0

Miller, A. (2022, October 21). Specright partners with Michigan State University School of Packaging to enhance student preparation for careers in the packaging industry. College of Agriculture & Natural Resources. Retrieved October 23, 2022, from https://www.canr.msu.edu/

Peele, S. (2022, October 10). HOME. Woodlawn School. Retrieved October 23, 2022, from https://woodlawnschool.org/

Invest in Real Estate. Do What Matters. (2022, September 21). Coach Carson. Retrieved October 23, 2022, from https://www.coachcarson.com/

https://en.wikipedia.org/wiki/Stingray_City,_Grand_Cayman